BEATING THE BLU

A self-help approach to overcom

CW00499070

SUSAN TANNER AND JILLIAN clinical psychologists. They have successfully treated hundreds of depressed people at the Prince Henry Hospital, Sydney, Australia, using the techniques described in *Beating the Blues*. Jillian Ball currently specializes in the treatment of depression, anxiety, eating disorders and relationship problems at Prince Henry Hospital. Susan Tanner is now in private practice, specializing in anxiety management, treatment of depression, social skills and assertiveness training.

Overcoming Common Problems Series

The ABC of Eating
Coping with anorexia, bulimia and compulsive eating
JOY MELVILLE

An A–Z of Alternative Medicine
BRENT Q. HAFEN AND KATHRYN J. FRANDSEN

Arthritis
Is your suffering really necessary?
DR WILLIAM FOX

Being the Boss
STEPHEN FITZSIMON

Birth Over Thirty
SHEILA KITZINGER

Body Language
How to read others' thoughts by their gestures
ALLAN PEASE

Bodypower
DR VERNON COLEMAN

Calm Down
How to cope with frustration and anger
DR PAUL HAUCK

Comfort for Depression
JANET HORWOOD

Common Childhood Illnesses
DR PATRICIA GILBERT

Complete Public Speaker
GYLES BRANDRETH

Coping with Anxiety and Depression
SHIRLEY TRICKETT

Coping with Depression and Elation
DR PATRICK McKEON

Coping with Stress
DR GEORGIA WITKIN-LANOIL

Coping with Suicide
DR DONALD SCOTT

Coping with Thrush
CAROLINE CLAYTON

Coping Successfully with Your Child's Asthma
DR PAUL CARSON

Coping Successfully with Your Child's Skin Problems
DR PAUL CARSON

Coping Successfully with Your Hyperactive Child
DR PAUL CARSON

Coping Successfully with Your Irritable Bowel
ROSEMARY NICOL

Curing Arthritis Cookbook
MARGARET HILLS

Curing Arthritis – The Drug-free Way
MARGARET HILLS

Curing Coughs, Colds and Flu – the Drug-free Way
MARGARET HILLS

Curing Illness – The Drug-free Way
MARGARET HILLS

Depression
DR PAUL HAUCK

Divorce and Separation
ANGELA WILLANS

The Dr Moerman Cancer Diet
RUTH JOCHEMS

The Epilepsy Handbook
SHELAGH McGOVERN

Everything You Need to Know about Adoption
MAGGIE JONES

Everything You Need to Know about Contact Lenses
DR ROBERT YOUNGSON

Everything You Need to Know about Your Eyes
DR ROBERT YOUNGSON

Everything You Need to Know about the Pill
WENDY COOPER AND TOM SMITH

Everything You Need to Know about Shingles
DR ROBERT YOUNGSON

Family First Aid and Emergency Handbook
DR ANDREW STANWAY

Feverfew
A traditional herbal remedy for migraine and arthritis
DR STEWART JOHNSON

Overcoming Common Problems Series

Fight Your Phobia and Win
DAVID LEWIS

Flying Without Fear
TESSA DUCKWORTH AND DAVID MILLER

Goodbye Backache
DR DAVID IMRIE WITH COLLEEN DIMSON

Good Publicity Guide
REGINALD PEPLOW

Helping Children Cope with Divorce
ROSEMARY WELLS

Helping Children Cope with Grief
ROSEMARY WELLS

How to Be Your Own Best Friend
DR PAUL HAUCK

How to Control your Drinking
DRS W. MILLER AND R. MUNOZ

How to Cope with Stress
DR PETER TYRER

How to Cope with your Child's Allergies
DR PAUL CARSON

How to Cope with your Nerves
DR TONY LAKE

How to Cope with Tinnitus and Hearing Loss
DR ROBERT YOUNGSON

How to Cure Your Ulcer
ANNE CHARLISH AND DR BRIAN GAZZARD

How to Do What You Want to Do
DR PAUL HAUCK

How to Enjoy Your Old Age
DR B. F. SKINNER AND M. E. VAUGHAN

How to Improve Your Confidence
DR KENNETH HAMBLY

How to Interview and Be Interviewed
MICHELE BROWN AND GYLES BRANDRETH

How to Love a Difficult Man
NANCY GOOD

How to Love and be Loved
DR PAUL HAUCK

How to Make Successful Decisions
ALISON HARDINGHAM

How to Pass Your Driving Test
DONALD RIDLAND

How to Say No to Alcohol
KEITH McNEILL

How to Sleep Better
DR PETER TYRER

How to Stand up for Yourself
DR PAUL HAUCK

How to Start a Conversation and Make Friends
DON GABOR

How to Stop Feeling Guilty
DR VERNON COLEMAN

How to Stop Smoking
GEORGE TARGET

How to Stop Taking Tranquillisers
DR PETER TYRER

Hysterectomy
SUZIE HAYMAN

If Your Child is Diabetic
JOANNE ELLIOTT

Jealousy
DR PAUL HAUCK

Learning to Live with Multiple Sclerosis
DR ROBERT POVEY, ROBIN DOWIE AND GILLIAN PRETT

Living Alone – A Woman's Guide
LIZ McNEILL TAYLOR

Living with Grief
DR TONY LAKE

Living Through Personal Crisis
ANN KAISER STEARNS

Living with High Blood Pressure
DR TOM SMITH

Loneliness
DR TONY LAKE

Making Marriage Work
DR PAUL HAUCK

Overcoming Common Problems Series

Making the Most of Loving
GILL COX AND SHEILA DAINOW

Making the Most of Yourself
GILL COX AND SHEILA DAINOW

Making Relationships Work
CHRISTINE SANDFORD AND WYN BEARDSLEY

Managing Two Careers
How to survive as a working mother
PATRICIA O'BRIEN

Meeting People is Fun
How to overcome shyness
DR PHYLLIS SHAW

The Nervous Person's Companion
DR KENNETH HAMBLY

One Parent Families
DIANA DAVENPORT

Overcoming Fears and Phobias
A woman's guide
DR TONY WHITEHEAD

Overcoming Shyness
DIANNE DOUBTFIRE

Overcoming Stress
DR VERNON COLEMAN

Overcoming Tension
DR KENNETH HAMBLY

Overcoming Your Nerves
DR TONY LAKE

The Parkinson's Disease Handbook
DR RICHARD GODWIN-AUSTEN

Say When!
Everything a woman needs to know about alcohol and drinking problems
ROSEMARY KENT

Second Wife, Second Best?
Managing your marriage as a second wife
GLYNNIS WALKER

Self-Help for your Arthritis
EDNA PEMBLE

Six Weeks to a Healthy Back
ALEXANDER MELLEBY

Sleep Like a Dream – The Drug-Free Way
ROSEMARY NICOL

Solving your Personal Problems
PETER HONEY

Someone to Love
How to find romance in the personal columns
MARGARET NELSON

A Step-Parent's Handbook
KATE RAPHAEL

Stress and your Stomach
DR VERNON COLEMAN

Trying to Have a Baby?
Overcoming infertility and child loss
MAGGIE JONES

What Everyone Should Know about Drugs
KENNETH LEECH

Why Be Afraid?
How to overcome your fears
DR PAUL HAUCK

You and Your Varicose Veins
DR PATRICIA GILBERT

Your Arthritic Hip and You
GEORGE TARGET

Overcoming Common Problems

BEATING THE BLUES

A self-help approach to overcoming depression

Susan Tanner and Jillian Ball

Illustrations by Brian Kogler

SHELDON PRESS
LONDON

First published in Australia in 1989 by
Doubleday, a division of Transworld Publishers (Aust.) Pty Limited

First published in Great Britain 1989
Sheldon Press, SPCK, Marylebone Road, London NW1 4DU
by arrangement with Transworld Publishers (Aust.) Pty Limited

© Susan Tanner and Jillian Ball 1989

All rights reserved. No part of this book may be reproduced or transmitted in any form or by any means, electronic or mechanical, including photocopying, recording, or by any information storage and retrieval system, without permission in writing from the publisher.

British Library Cataloguing in Publication Data

Tanner, Susan
Beating the blues. – (Overcoming common problems).
1. Man. Depression. Therapy. Self-help – Manuals
I. Title II. Series
616.85′2706

ISBN 0–85969–601–4

Printed in Great Britain by Biddles Ltd, Guildford and Kings Lynn

To our patients who generously shared their experiences, time and energy.

Contents

Acknowledgements

The authors wish to thank Brian Kogler, Rae Ball, Kerrie Eyers, Pam Harris, Robert Kaplan, Stephen Kirkman, Noel Uhe, Lindy Wright and staff at the Mood Disorders Unit, Prince Henry Hospital for their valuable suggestions and support.

We would also like to thank our families, partners and friends for feeding us while we created and our patients who contributed their personal stories and experiences.

Thanks also to Anne Pender and Anne Kern.

Beating the Blues is a joint effort. The order of authorship does not imply order of seniority or contribution.

INTRODUCTION

Is This Book for You?

- Are you fed up with particular aspects of your life?
- Have you lost the ability to enjoy things that used to give you pleasure?
- Do you wake up in the morning and wonder how you will get through the day?
- Do you feel that your concentration and memory are not as good as they used to be?
- Do you dwell on feelings of failure and hopelessness?
- Does your future seem bleak?

If you answered yes to some of these questions, you are not alone. The blues and depression are surprisingly common in our society. At any one time, one in five adults is feeling down and one in ten is showing more significant signs of depression. In fact depression has been described as the common cold of the psyche.[1]

This book is for people–

- who are dissatisfied with their lives, but don't know what to change.
- who are fed up and blue and can't seem to snap out of it.
- who are interested in learning how to control and prevent unpleasant emotions such as depression, anxiety, loneliness, jealousy and hopelessness.
- who wish to build up their self-confidence and self-esteem.
- who wish to know how to help friends or family members suffering from depression.

By understanding the relationship between your thoughts and your moods, you will see how thinking in certain ways puts you at risk of feeling blue or suffering more intense depression. This book teaches you how to modify your moods by changing your thinking style.

By becoming aware of your thinking habits, you will be able to react more spontaneously to situations. You will have greater

HO-HUM...
NOT ANOTHER BOOK ABOUT OVERCOMING THE GLUMS!
I'LL BET THE LAST PAGE IS MISSING...

choice in how you react to events instead of being tied to old habits and hampered by unwanted feelings. You will have better self-control.

Case Histories

Throughout the book, we have included letters and stories from people who have come to us for help in overcoming depression. In particular, we shall follow the progress of five people suffering from various types of depression:

KATHERINE is a 35 year old mother of two children who came to us after she had been depressed for six months. She had felt down before, but not like this. She was constantly restless and tired and had difficulty getting to sleep at night. She suffered from severe stomach pains but no physical cause could be found. At times she feared that something was seriously wrong with her body.

Katherine had a happy childhood. She had a good relationship with her younger sister and felt that her parents were supportive and interested in her welfare. She completed a business studies course after leaving school and pursued a career as a sales consultant. She married at the age of 18 and separated a few years later. In her late twenties, Katherine married again and enjoyed some happy and fulfilling years. She had two children in her second marriage and gave up her job after the second baby was born. She was busy and happy caring for the children. However, when her younger child started school, things started to change. Katherine became bored and felt that life lacked purpose. She felt encumbered by household tasks. She desperately missed the sense of achievement that she had previously experienced through her work. Her husband, on the other hand, was doing well in his business and was spending less time at home. She pleaded with him to show more interest in the family and to give more assistance with disciplining the children. Arguments became frequent and heated.

It was about this time that Katherine became depressed. She lost interest in her old pleasures and became irritable with everyone. She wept for long periods. She was considering separation, but this decision, along with all others, seemed too difficult for her to make. She lost confidence in herself and in her decisions.

Katherine was admitted to our depression programme feeling helpless about dealing with the stresses that she was facing. She was also concerned about becoming dependent on medication.

DAVID is a 50 year old finance manager, married with a teenage son. He had a chronic depression that began several years ago. He felt unhappy and lethargic. Sometimes he suffered more intense episodes, when he felt deep despair and became highly anxious and agitated. Unlike some depressed people, he overslept and ate too much when feeling down. He craved sweet foods and gained weight during these times. He had suicidal thoughts from time to time, and he questioned the point of going on. Fishing was one of the few activities which gave him pleasure. He described himself as a loner.

When his depression developed, he could not see any clear reasons for it. At this time, he noticed that he was becoming irritable and aggressive towards his wife and son even though he loved and cared for them. David was frightened by his lack of control. He became even more distressed when he noticed that his son was taking on similar aggressive characteristics.

David had always been a perfectionist, setting extraordinarily high standards for others as well as himself. This had been useful in his work and he had recently been promoted to the position of finance manager in a large bank. To a degree he thrived on the pressures of his job, yet he was fearful that he would not be able to cope with the increasing responsibilities. He worked excessively hard and was highly sensitive to criticism. Despite extensive trials of medication, he remained anxious and depressed. He came to us keen to learn some self-control techniques.

MICHELLE is a 28 year old teacher who lives alone. She had been suffering from depressive episodes on and off since adolescence. Michelle was close to her mother and they both had difficulty getting through a day without repeated contact with each other. During her teenage years she had a stormy relationship with her father. She held him in awe, yet she felt that she never received enough affection from him. Michelle was a very bright girl, who did well at school, but felt that she had not received as much recognition as had her two brothers.

Michelle had a relationship with a married man for some months, but felt that it was unsatisfactory. She has a few friends but has not allowed them to get too close for fear that they would reject her if they really got to know her.

PETER is a 19 year old unemployed youth, referred to us by his family doctor who had known him since he was born. It was mainly because of his doctor's concern that Peter's depression was identified and he was encouraged to seek help.

Peter came from a family of four children. He left school after completing his School Certificate and worked in various jobs. When we met him he had been unemployed for 10 months. Although he left his parents' home for a while, he had been forced to return, because he could not afford to pay his own rent and bills.

Peter's parents noticed that since returning home, he had become more and more withdrawn, had stopped seeing a lot of his friends and had lost interest in his usual hobbies of tinkering with his car, listening to bands and surfing. Most days he would stay in bed until the early afternoon. He would also just sit for hours, daydreaming.

Along with many of his co-workers, Peter was laid off from his job as an apprentice. For the following three to four months he had tried to get other jobs. However, as time went on he had become more and more demoralised.

His parents tried to talk to him about their concern for him, but he would snap at them and leave the house. There was usually an argument with his father when he returned. Peter's behaviour was creating a lot of stress within the family and this, in turn, was causing him to feel worse. Because Peter could not talk about his feelings, he would bottle things up and so seemed to become unreachable. He began to treat his girlfriend badly, which she couldn't understand, so she stopped seeing him.

When Peter came to us, his self-confidence was at rock bottom. He hated himself, and believed that his family and friends hated him too.

RUTH is a 67 year old woman whose husband, Harry, had died of dementia five months earlier. The course of Harry's illness was 10 years. Eventually, he became dependent on Ruth for everything. They had been married for forty years and had a loving relationship. They had three children and five grandchildren.

During the initial stages of Harry's illness, Ruth attempted to shield the family from his difficulties and did not ask for any help or support. She had always been an independent, self-reliant and practical woman and found it hard to ask for help. Ruth's role during the last few years of Harry's life was to devote herself completely to caring for him. She no longer played bowls and rarely contacted old friends. Harry became increasingly hard to manage and at times she felt overwhelmed, confused and frustrated. She kept these feelings to herself and felt guilty if she left his side.

After Harry's death, Ruth stayed at her daughter's home for some weeks. This made the grief seem easier to bear. However, after a while she felt that she should go back to her own home and not impose on her daughter's family any longer. On returning home Ruth became profoundly lonely and felt that there was no meaning left in her life. Initially she attempted to keep up with routine household tasks but even this became difficult. She lost her appetite and had problems with motivating herself to leave the house to do the shopping. Her concentration was poor and she had trouble remembering simple things. She was frightened about what would happen to her if she was unable to care for herself and lay awake at night fearing what her future would be like alone.

Ruth discussed her fears with some friends, who encouraged her to seek professional help.

Cognitive Behaviour Therapy: How Does it Work?

The techniques described in this book are based on a treatment approach known as Cognitive Behaviour Therapy (or simply Cognitive Therapy) developed by Aaron Beck and Albert Ellis.[2] The theory is that the way people think about themselves and the world around them contributes to the development and maintenance of intense unpleasant feelings.

Behaviour therapy aims to change your behaviour, so that your attitudes and moods are modified. Cognitive Therapy teaches you how to change your thinking habits so that you feel better by using the following simple process:

1 You are guided in identifying your negative thoughts.
2 You learn how to detect the distortions in your thinking and how to challenge and correct them.
3 You are shown how to generate more positive thoughts and beliefs which will enhance your self-esteem.

This approach teaches you how to change your behaviour by setting daily and weekly goals. By attempting activities that are challenging, you are able to build self-confidence and encourage personal growth.

How to Get the Best from this Book

This book offers practical suggestions and a step by step guide to a very successful programme for change. A series of exercises and techniques are outlined which are useful tools in the process

of gaining control over your moods. They are carefully worked out and are an integral part of the cognitive therapy approach. To get maximum benefit from the book, you need to do the suggested exercises.

- Put these techniques into practice regularly.
- Make working towards change a high priority. Try not to make excuses, forget to practise or do the exercises half-heartedly.
- Tackle your problems one at a time. This will make it easier to get started and stop you from being overwhelmed.
- Be persistent and patient. It takes time to change and develop mastery over new skills.
- Believe that you can change!
- Motivate yourself by asking the following questions:

What are the advantages of being more in control of my moods?
What are the advantages of starting now rather than later?
Do I have anything to lose by trying this approach?

- Expect lapses and forgive yourself for them. It takes time to change habits that you may have had for many years.
- If you are having difficulty applying the techniques, ask yourself whether you are putting in enough effort each day to change and if you are expecting too much too soon.

Feeling Better and Getting Better

Simply knowing what to do does not mean you will always be able to do it! If you have suffered with severe levels of anxiety or depression in the past, it is important for you to understand that getting better does not follow a smooth, upward progress curve, but rather a bumpy one. If you have a bad day or two in the future, it is not a sign that you are getting worse and that the techniques do not work! You can bounce back after a rough patch without letting it become a deep depression.

David Burns,[3] a leading proponent of Cognitive Therapy, draws attention to the difference between feeling better and getting better. Feeling better can occur spontaneously or with medications. However, in most cases, getting better results from systematically applying and re-applying self-control techniques that will lift your mood and change unhelpful reactions whenever the need arises. You will then be better equipped to cope with the ups and downs of everyday life and be a healthier, more self-respecting person.

We know that the techniques in this book work and we hope that you will enjoy finding this out for yourself!

Chapter 1

UNDERSTANDING DEPRESSION

'I saw that all things that I feared and which feared me had nothing good or bad about them save insofar as the mind was affected by them.'

SPINOZA

People experience depression in different ways.

'When I'm feeling depressed I can't be bothered doing anything. I just want to stay in bed and avoid everyone and everything.'

(MICHELLE)

'For me it is like having a great weight on my shoulders. It is as if I am fighting my way through a thick blinding mist and have become lost. Sometimes I don't feel that I'm able to keep fighting.'

(DAVID)

'When I'm depressed, I feel that I am no one anymore. My inside is like an empty pit. All I want to do is to curl up and disappear. I can't face anyone—I don't want them to see me crying like this. I feel so frightened. If only I had measles or a broken leg—I could accept that more.'

(KATHERINE)

'I get so lonely sometimes. I hear the clock tick and listen to the time pass so slowly and just wish that the day would hurry up and finish.'

(RUTH)

Normal Moods

Moods are an important part of our everyday experiences and add a certain richness to the quality of life. From time to time everyone feels 'down' or 'fed up' or 'out of sorts'. Sadness, concern, disappointment and annoyance can be useful emotional responses to situations that did not turn out the way you would have liked them to. These feelings are often a message that some effort is required to readjust, or that something constructive must be done to deal with your feelings or to change the situation.

Depression

Many people will experience more marked distressing feelings at some time during their life. Depression lasts longer than sadness and the blues and the accompanying feelings of helplessness, hopelessness and indecisiveness are often considerable.

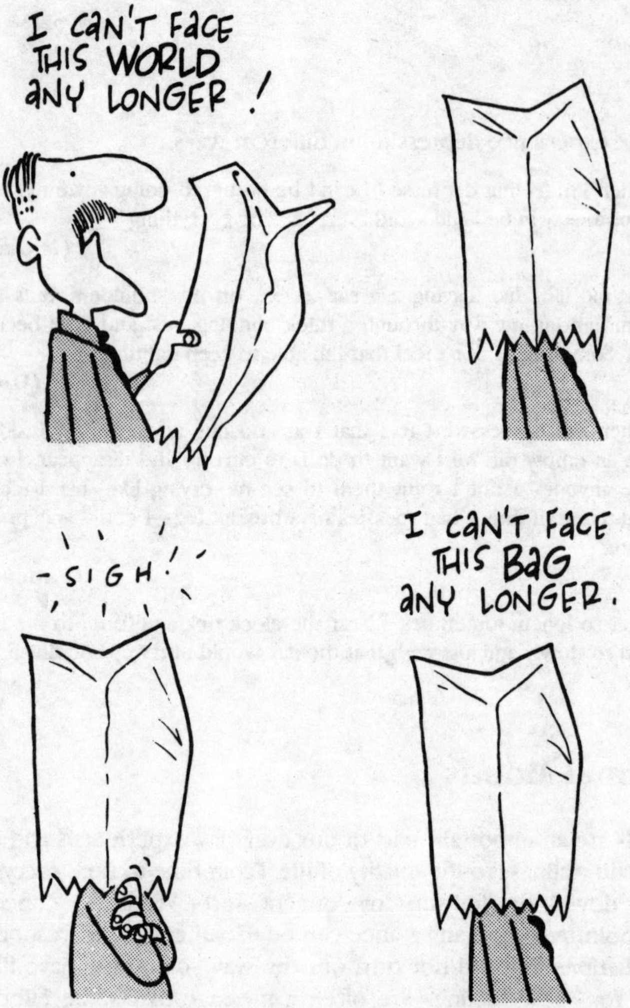

Recognising the Symptoms of Depression

Feeling depressed involves a wide range of symptoms which are different for each individual both in nature and severity. Noticeable changes in some of the following areas may indicate the presence of a depression:

Mood

—feeling sad, moody, gloomy or dispirited
—feeling irritable and unable to cope with everyday demands
—feeling guilty and blaming yourself
—feeling dead or numb emotionally
—inability to experience pleasure
—anxiety
—dreading everyday activities
—experiencing despair

Thinking

—seeing yourself in a much poorer light
—being overly self-critical
—blaming yourself for doing dreadful things
—believing that your depression is a punishment for past wrongs
—negative expectations and doubts about the future
—believing that you can't cope and that things are out of your control
—experiencing difficulty making decisions and thinking clearly
—thinking of suicide or other destructive activities, even planning how you might act out such urges
—imagining that others are putting you down and are out to get you
—poor concentration and memory

Behaviour

—decrease in activities
—lack of energy and motivation
—weepiness or difficulty in crying if you want to
—agitation and inability to stick at things for very long
—sluggishness
—social withdrawal or dependency on people
—increased use of drugs or alcohol

Physical Health

—loss of appetite leading to weight loss
—over-eating or food cravings
—disturbed sleep patterns—waking up during the night and being unable to get back to sleep, difficulty falling asleep or increased sleep
—loss of interest in sexual activities
—aches, pains and gastro-intestinal problems
—menstrual irregularities
—feeling physically ill

Types of Depression

Hippocrates (460-377 BC) was one of the first to challenge the belief that disorders of the mind were due to actions by the gods. Certain terms, such as *melancholia*, were derived from his ideas.

Since then, there have been repeated attempts to categorise and label different moods. However, it has not yet been conclusively established whether various depressions are actually different in type, or whether they differ only in severity.

This chapter provides guidelines on seven categories of depression, referring to the terms that doctors often use.

Limitations of Labelling: We recognise that categorising depressions may oversimplify them and not give sufficient emphasis to specific social, psychological and biological factors. However, categorising can be helpful if it gives you some ideas about treating your depression.

Reactive Depression

This type of depression may be the result of something traumatic that happens, or a series of problems which cause your stress levels to rise. After the source of the stress has been dealt with, the depression soon lifts. Depending on the nature of the stressor, the depression may last for a few days or weeks, while occasionally it is more prolonged.

Chronic Depression

When people experience a more longstanding type of depressive mood, it is often due to ongoing difficulties in coping with stress, low self-esteem, or unhelpful attitudes developed in childhood. People with chronic depressions tend to be overly aware of their mistakes and weaknesses and frequently put themselves down.

There are a variety of symptoms associated with this type of depression, but mostly the person feels helpless and pessimistic. Difficulty in going to sleep is often described, and evenings are generally the worst time, because this is when the perceived failures of the day are reviewed over and over in the person's mind.

Endogenous Depression

This type of depression involves biochemical changes in the brain. It is referred to as 'endogenous' because it appears to develop a life of its own. Often there are no obvious triggers. However, many health professionals now believe that in addition to the biochemical changes, unresolved problems and a build up of stress also contribute to this depression. Endogenous depression has a characteristic set of symptoms:

- There is a depressed mood with feelings of hopelessness, despair, worthlessness, guilt and a sense that the mood will never lift.
- The person does not feel better when encouraged by others or when pleasant events occur.
- The pattern of sleep disturbance typically involves waking up early, generally two to three hours before the usual time of waking, with difficulty getting back to sleep.
- People often notice that their mood improves as the day progresses, so the evenings are the best time for them.
- Marked bodily symptoms may occur including loss of appetite, constipation, extreme agitation, slowing down of thoughts and bodily movements and loss of interest in sexual activity. Some women also report disturbances to their menstrual cycle.
- In severe forms of the depression, delusions and hallucinations may occur. For example, some people believe that the insides of their body have rotted. Some people hear voices talking about them saying how bad and worthless they are. These experiences are quite distressing.
- Depressive episodes may come on over days or weeks and may last for months and occasionally for years. There may be times between episodes when there is some relief from the depression.

Manic-Depressive Illness

Manic-depressive illness involves cycles alternating between depression and mania. During a 'manic' episode the person becomes over-active and feels elated or 'high'. This feeling is more intense than in normal happiness and the mood is not responsive to what is happening at the time.

The manic episode may end abruptly, sometimes with the onset of a depression. During the depressive episodes symptoms are generally severe with intense feelings of worthlessness, self-reproach and withdrawal. Often there are periods of stability between mood swings. Episodes vary in length and severity, generally lasting for a few weeks or a few months. The onset of a manic-depressive illness is most common when people are in their twenties.

The cause of manic-depressive illness is still not fully understood. However, there is increasing evidence that it involves some changes in the body's biochemistry. Stressful life events are also known to trigger such episodes.

A number of famous and creative people are thought to have experienced manic-depressive mood swings. They include Abraham Lincoln, Sylvia Plath, Virginia Woolf and Vivienne Leigh.

There have been significant advances in the medical treatment of manic-depressive illness. In the 1950s, an Australian psychiatrist, Dr. John Cade, discovered that a salt, lithium carbonate, has a beneficial effect in the treatment of mania.

Life on a roller coaster: Dianne is a 32 year old single woman who works part-time as a research assistant. Her first depressive episode occurred when she was travelling overseas seven years ago. She then swung into a manic episode and was started on lithium.

> During my 'highs', I don't feel the need for sleep and get a rush of great ideas of how I could become wealthy and famous quickly. I have also spent money on things that I would not normally buy and have given large amounts of money away because I thought that I could afford to (which I couldn't). During one 'high' I ran up an enormous telephone bill without being aware of what I was doing, and apparently I became angry if anyone tried to stop me. My perception of colours and sounds has also intensified, and I have thought that I had the power to control the weather.
>
> After I had been on medication for a while I was able to get off the worst of the 'roller coaster', but my confidence had plummeted. I eventually realised that accepting my manic-depressive illness doesn't mean sitting back and just letting it happen again. I now try to anticipate my mood swings and to seek help before things get out of control.

Cyclothymia

For some people mood changes are more extreme than normal. They have mood swings from depression to elation with normal periods in between. When this occurs it is sometimes referred to as 'cyclothymia'. The swings are not extreme enough to be considered a manic-depressive illness, but cyclothymia, nevertheless, can interfere with everyday life, especially close relationships. Families may find it difficult to cope with someone who alternates between feeling helpless, inadequate and lethargic on some occasions, to being an over-active, over-confident person who requires little sleep, some time later.

Secondary Depressions

Depressions that are part of a medical illness or other psychiatric disorders are called 'secondary depressions'. The depression is not just a reaction to the illness, but is a part of the disease. The symptoms vary according to the nature of the disorder. Triggering factors include:

- Physical problems such as vitamin deficiencies, endocrine disease, viral infections (such as influenza, glandular fever and hepatitis), chronic fatigue syndrome, Parkinson's disease, Huntington's disease, cancer, thyroid disease and strokes.
- Excessive alcohol consumption or the taking of illicit drugs.
- Psychiatric disorders such as schizophrenia.
- Medications including blood pressure tablets and steroids.

Disorders Which Mimic Depression

There are other disorders which mimic depression. The most common is dementia which involves a progressive deterioration of intellectual abilities due to cells dying in the brain. Symptoms include memory problems, especially for recent events, difficulties with organising and learning new information, logical reasoning and abstract thinking. Dementia sufferers become less able to make sound judgements socially and at work and they often have trouble communicating effectively. People with these problems in functioning often become withdrawn and depressed, especially in the early stages of the disease. The onset of dementia is most common when people are 60 years or older, but it may occur much earlier.

Cognitive Therapy and the Different Types of Depression

Cognitive Therapy aims for more self-control over thoughts and feelings. It is an effective treatment for many different types of emotional difficulties.

The intensity, duration and frequency of unhelpful emotions can be reduced by learning to put situations into perspective and setting realistic goals for the future. Long-term attitudes which had led to distress can also be challenged. This will in turn increase feelings of self-esteem. Cognitive Therapy is especially valuable in treating reactive and chronic depressions.

Cognitive Therapy can also be effective in the treatment of some endogeneous depressions. Sometimes people who develop biological depressions have had good coping strategies in the past, but their thinking becomes negative and illogical when they are depressed. Unhelpful attitudes and stress may also contribute to the onset of biological depressions. It is valuable to challenge these unhelpful changes in thinking before they become habits.

Accepting and learning to live with manic-depressive illness and cyclothymia can be difficult psychological hurdles. Cognitive

Therapy can help people to cope with and control their mood swings and assist them to reach their individual potential.

Secondary depressions and disorders which mimic depression must be investigated and treated medically. Cognitive Therapy is not designed to alleviate the symptoms underlying these disorders.

Rating Your Moods

Keeping track of the nature and severity of your moods will help you to understand more about yourself. Use the following scale to record your mood changes.

EXERCISE 1

Instructions: Listed below are nine thoughts, feelings and symptoms people may have when they are feeling depressed. Please rate how you are currently feeling by placing an (X) on each of the lines at the position on the line best reflecting how you feel.

EXAMPLE:

I do not feel cold	——————X——————	I feel as cold as is possible

1 I do not feel unhappy at all	____________________	I feel so sad that I can't stand it
2 I get as much pleasure from things as usual	____________________	I get no pleasure from doing things
3 I look forward to pleasurable events	____________________	I am unable to look forward to things
4 I do not feel guilty	____________________	I feel as guilty as possible
5 I do not feel unworthy	____________________	I feel totally unworthy
6 I do not feel slowed down physically	____________________	I feel completely slowed down physically

7 My thoughts come easily	________________	I find it impossible to think at all
8 I do not feel anxious	________________	I am as anxious as anyone can be
9 I have as much energy as usual	________________	I have no energy at all

Visual Analogue Scale — Boyce (1987)

Using the scale: Compare your results before and after applying the techniques in this book, and each week complete the scale again.

Chapter 2

WHAT MAKES PEOPLE VULNERABLE TO DEPRESSION

'He who conquers others is strong;
He who conquers himself is mighty.'
LAO TSE *(c. 6014–531 BC)*

This chapter sheds light on why some people are more prone to the blues and depression than others and examines factors which trigger depression in susceptible individuals.

Coping Strategies

Consider this situation. Two people have been told that they have diabetes. The first man is distraught. He blames his condition on factors beyond his control and thinks that there is little he can do to help himself. He believes that all the good times in life are now behind him. He ignores the dietary advice given to him and withdraws angrily from his family and friends. He becomes resentful of their good health.

The second man is dismayed with the news of his diabetes, but immediately tries to find out what he can do about his health problem. He realises that his condition is largely due to problems in his lifestyle and diet and makes plans to alter these aspects of his daily life. He recognises that he has been working hard at the expense of his health and plans some leisure activities. He discusses his concerns with his family and gains their support in making changes.

The responses of these people to the same situation are clearly quite different. The differences reflect their 'coping strategies'.

Coping strategies are the reactions you have to stressful situations. Good coping strategies protect you from distressing feelings. Poor coping strategies place you at risk of becoming depressed or anxious.

What Determines Your Coping Strategies?

Your ability to cope is influenced by psychological factors such as whether or not you like yourself, how well you relate to others, whether you are a realistic thinker, how you interpret changes in your body, whether you are able to admit to having problems and what type of personality you have. These six determinants are enlarged on under the following headings:

1 Self-esteem

Values, attitudes and rules learnt as a child become part of your individual thinking style. These beliefs have a direct bearing on how you judge your behaviour and achievements. The term 'self-esteem' refers to how you feel about yourself. This is one of the main factors which determines how you will ride the ups and downs of everyday life and cope with extra stresses.

High self-esteem comes from liking yourself and acknowledging your strengths as well as your weaknesses. It helps you to deal constructively with criticism, rejection and conflict without blaming yourself unnecessarily and puts you in a better position to develop good coping strategies.

Low self-esteem is usually caused by unrealistic personal values and beliefs that are difficult to live by. For example, if you grew up with a very critical parent, you may believe you need the approval of people you care about in order to feel worthwhile. This belief will cause difficulty in handling criticism and will lower your self-esteem.

2 Assertion and Social Skills

An ability to communicate effectively with others and to express your needs and feelings directly allows you to manage your life better. If you bottle up emotions or feel out of control when you express them, then you will be less effective in your attempts to deal with stresses and conflicts with others. The ability to be assertive is determined by your attitudes towards, yourself and others and by your opportunities to, practise such skills.

Developing close relationships and trusting others also improves your strategies for coping. Talking things through can help to put problems into perspective and find solutions. It is also very important to strike the right balance between dependence and independence in relying on social supports. Developing trusting relationships and expressing your needs and wishes directly are behaviours which can be learnt.

3 Thinking Habits

How you feel and what you do are affected by the way you interpret events. Good coping strategies are based on logical and realistic thoughts which help you to set goals to overcome difficulties. For example, 'I'm concerned and frightened that I have diabetes, but I'll try to improve my health to see if that improves the situation'. Poor coping strategies occur when you overreact to a situation by exaggerated and illogical thinking: 'This is just too much, I can't handle it'.

4 Interpretation of Your Physical Sensations

Your body is constantly undergoing physiological changes and your mind's task is to interpret these changes and explain them to yourself. At times you may interpret certain physical symptoms such as a pounding heart as due to fear, at other times, excitement. If you think that your physical states are due to depression, then you will probably feel depressed. People often mistakenly explain fatigue and temporary physical illness, such as the flu and prementrual tension, as a sign of depression and this can cause problems.

For example, one of the people we treated woke up with a dull headache and felt that he lacked motivation to do anything. He took these sensations to mean that he was depressed and subsequently felt defeated. When we questioned him more closely, we discovered that he had worked overtime several nights during the week and had been out socialising until early that morning, so he had good reason to be tired. Interestingly, when his symptoms were related to tiredness rather than depression, he felt considerably better.

Interpreting your physical sensations accurately and carefully will help you to avoid thinking yourself into a depression.

5 Accepting the Problem

Recognising and acknowledging that you have a problem is the important first step in doing something about it. Sometimes people attempt to deny or minimise their concerns and feelings. Other people build up or maximise their problems to the point where they feel overwhelmed by their distressing feelings.

You may find yourself taking on more and more activities to avoid facing unpleasant feelings, especially when you fear that they will overwhelm you. You may believe that you should not be feeling down because there is no good reason for it, or you see such feelings as a sign of weakness. Some people who have difficulty accepting that they are depressed, focus only on their physical symptoms, such as sleeping difficulties or fatigue.

'Maximising' your feelings of depression involves exaggerating their significance and giving in to your feelings without trying to overcome them. You become overly watchful, exaggerating every sensation and registering every change in body and mood, so that you become preoccupied with your internal states. This makes it difficult to respond to the situation constructively.

6 Personality Characteristics

Your attitudes and personal values give rise to certain personality characteristics, some of which put you at risk of becoming depressed. Contrary to belief, these characteristics are not fixed or unchanging, because they are based on thinking habits which can be modified. Personality characteristics affect your reactions to everyday stresses and life events. They are a double edged sword, in that a little is fine, but too much will hinder your coping abilities.

Apart from perfectionism which we will discuss later in Chapter 8, some personality qualities which put you at risk are:

Dependency—relying on others to look after you, to make you feel worthwhile and to provide you with motivation and direction. This leads to an over-sensitivity to criticism and rejection and a tendency to cling to people when you are distressed.

Conformity—adhering too closely to what others expect of you. You are frightened of deviating as you believe even minor variations will lead to disapproval.

Rigidity—means that you have firm opinions and are unable to consider other viewpoints. You are seen as inflexible and unfeeling. When other people express opinions or feelings different to your own, you feel uncomfortable and threatened.

You may find it interesting to find out more about your personality by filling out the questionnaire in Exercise 2 at the end of this chapter. This will indicate whether your personality characteristics place you at risk of becoming depressed.

How are Coping Strategies Learned?

Coping strategies are learned from your childhood experiences and the attitudes and expectations of your society and culture. These factors shape your behaviour and influence how you deal with stresses and the feelings which arise from them.

Parents, teachers and significant people in your early years teach you values and attitudes to live by. They do this by praising certain things that you do and punishing others. If you have been taught constructive attitudes you will be well equipped to foster a good opinion of yourself and deal with the demands of daily life. If you have been taught unhelpful attitudes then it is important that you become aware of them and adopt alternative ones.

When you follow social attitudes without questioning them, you lose your sense of identity. Trying to live by socially determined values may cause you to adopt a lifestyle that does not fulfil your own needs. For example, people sometimes feel pressured into becoming competitive and riding up a particular path in order to be seen to be successful. This may prevent them from developing their individual potential. Depression often occurs when you are trying to live up to what you think you should be, rather than what you could be.

The influence of social expectations is seen in the changing role of women in society. Thirty years ago women were expected to stay home to be good wives and mothers. Now there is more emphasis on women managing a career as well as a family. More women are placing excessive stress on themselves to satisfy the demands of their children, husband and career. Some of the women we have treated have complained that they feel pressured to go to work, as the role of housewife is less valued by society today.

The assumptions and expectations you have about others can cause vulnerability to depression. If you are flexible you will be able to adapt to a variety of people or situations. However, if your social attitudes are rigid and stereotyped they will have an adverse effect on your relationships with others. Examples of unhelpful traditional sex stereotypes are:

Women should not initiate relationships
Men shouldn't show their emotions

There are sex differences in people's attitudes towards seeking treatment. Twice as many women seek treatment for depression as men. When men are distressed they are more likely to abuse alcohol, withdraw or focus on physical symptoms.

Which Factors Trigger Depression?

Feelings of depression are most likely to arise during times of stress. Triggering events may be social, such as developmental crises, stressful life events, excessive stress and lifestyle problems; or biological, involving disturbances in your neurotransmitters, hormones or biological rhythms.

Social and Psychological Factors

• Developmental Crises

Throughout life, people progress through a predicted series of stages or 'crises'. Crises are life problems which demand more than routine coping. Each crisis provides an opportunity to learn more about yourself and to further develop your coping strategies. How societies react to the various developmental stages differs across cultures. The importance given to youth, for example, is a characteristic of western cultures. Other societies, such as the Chinese culture, have traditionally given more respect to the elderly.

Early crises: Adolescent crises involve separation from the family, leaving home, adjustments to bodily changes and attempts to

establish a sense of identity. Questions such as 'Who am I?' and 'What am I here for?' become major issues as decisions regarding appearance, friends and career are made. The biological, psychological and social changes experienced at puberty often trigger mood changes, irritability and depression.

Generally, the 20s focus more on intimate relationships and the pursuit of employment prospects. The 30s are sometimes described as the time of evaluation. Commitment in relationships, the decision whether to have a family, or make career changes, are all significant issues for some people at this time. Decisions made in the 20s are often reviewed and reflected upon and alternative values or paths pursued.

Middle crises: The developmental crises of the 40's and 50's are often overlooked by Western society. Adjustments may include menopause, the children leaving home and evaluation of achievements and goals of the 20's. The biological changes which occur with age, such as appearance and a reduced capacity for reproduction, can be difficult to cope with.

At this time roles may change within the family as children grow up. Opportunities for further advances at work may be limited. These factors can trigger the tendency to question what has been achieved. Feelings of insecurity about the future may emerge, accompanied by anxiety and depression. Some men have affairs with younger women at this stage to prove their vigour and youth. This process is often referred to as the 'mid-life crisis'.

How you react to these developmental issues is determined by your previous coping strategies, your sense of identity and your attitudes. Unless you re-establish goals and place emphasis on your own needs as opposed to social expectations, you may well feel disillusioned, bitter and resentful at missed opportunities.

Late crises: There is less written in popular literature about the developmental crises in later life. This stage can be a very rich and fulfilling one. Retirement provides increased time for other interests, such as travel, and contact with growing families and grandchildren. However, during this developmental stage, there is also the increased likelihood of certain crises including loss of physical health and the death of loved ones. Retirement for some people involves stressful readjustments and may be accompanied by loneliness and the perceived loss of usefulness and achievement. Coming to terms with this phase means placing less emphasis on achievements and productivity as a source of self-esteem and focusing on what you can enjoy and experience from the present. The inability to do so can lead to depressive feelings.

• Life events

The blues and depression may be triggered by unpredictable events which involve a change in daily living. Situations which signal major changes in routine are called 'life events'. Examples include starting a new job, breaking up of a relationship, death or illness in the family or financial difficulties. Life events can be pleasant (job promotion) or unpleasant (retrenchment). Such events give you the opportunity to learn more about yourself and are important for your development as a person. However, they are also the times when you are most susceptible to emotional turmoil.

Childbirth and the subsequent role adjustments are a significant source of stress for both the mother and the father. Up to 20% of women experience a post-natal depression in the first six months following childbirth.[1] Post-natal depression generally involves an interplay of biological, psychological and social factors.

MARY, a 26 year old woman, came to us with a post-natal depression three months after giving birth to twins. Her depression was triggered by more than just hormonal changes. She had recently faced a series of life events, including moving to a new city, separation from her family and friends, and adjustments to her new full-time role as mother. In addition to feeling overwhelmed by the emotional and physical adjustments, Mary also had various unrealistic expectations of herself. For instance, she believed that:

'It is a sign of weakness to show my feelings or to ask for help.'
'I must be a perfect mother and never feel irritable with my children.'

In overcoming her depression, Mary learnt to have more realistic expectations of herself in her new roles. She also learnt that expressing her feelings and seeking help during difficult times is a strength and not a weakness.

Life events are unavoidable. However, becoming depressed in response to the stress may be prevented. In fact most people who experience significant stressors do not become depressed. Sometimes people experience depression when there is no obvious prior stressful life event. Such feelings may be the result of years of unhappiness, ongoing relationship problems, unresolved conflict or a delayed reaction to something that happened a long time ago.

Complete Exercise 3 to determine the stressors currently in your life.

EXERCISE 3

Life Events Questionnaire

This questionnaire, devised by Tennant and Andrews (1976), covers a wide range of desirable and undesirable life events. The first column 'Distress' measures the amount of emotional stress caused by the event. The second column 'Life Change' measures the magnitude of changes to your routine.

Instructions:

Circle any of the following events you have experienced over the past 12 months.

	Event	Distress scalings	Life change scalings
HEALTH (Men and Women)			
1	You had a minor illness or injury like one needing a visit to a doctor or a couple of days off work	2	2
2	You had a serious illness, injury or operation needing hospitalization or a month or more off work	16	16
3	A close relative had a serious illness (from which they did not die)	16	9
	(Women Only)		
4	You are pregnant (with a wanted pregnancy)	2	26

	Event	Distress scalings	Life change scalings
5	You are pregnant (with an unwanted pregnancy)	33	29
6	You had a stillbirth	40	22
7	You had an abortion or miscarriage	26	13
8	You had a baby	5	47
9	Your change of life (menopause) began	14	18
10	You adopted a child	4	47
	(Men Only)		
11	Your wife had a child or you adopted a child	4	41
BEREAVEMENT (Men and Women)			
12	Your wife/husband died	83	79
13	A child of yours died	80	57
14	A close family member died (e.g. parent, brother, etc)	57	27
15	A close family friend or relative died (e.g. Aunt, Uncle, Grandmother, Cousin, etc)	30	12
FAMILY AND SOCIAL (If you are or were married)			
16	You married	5	59
17	There has been increasing serious arguments with your wife/husband	26	25
18	There has been a marked improvement in the way you and your wife/husband are getting on	2	18
19	You have been separated from your husband/wife for more than a month because of marital difficulties	31	29
20	You have been separated from your wife/husband for more than a month (for reasons other than marital difficulties)	12	15
21	You have got back together again after a separation due to marital difficulties	5	25
22	You began an extramarital affair	14	28
23	Your wife/husband began an extramarital affair	35	28
24	You have been divorced	54	62
	(If you have or had children)		
25	A child of yours became engaged	2	6
26	A child of yours married with your approval	2	10
27	A child of yours married without your approval	22	16
28	A child of yours left home for reasons other than marriage	11	14
29	A child of yours entered the armed services	9	10
	(If you are single)		
30	You became engaged or began a 'steady' relationship	2	17
31	You broke off your engagement	25	21
32	You broke off a 'steady' relationship	18	18

	Event	Distress scalings	Life change scalings
33	You had increasing arguments or difficulties with your fiance or steady friend	15	13
FRIENDS AND RELATIVES			
34	A new person came to live in your household (apart from a new baby)	8	20
35	There has been a marked improvement in the way you get on with someone close to you (excluding husband and wife)	1	10
36	You have been separated from someone important to you (other than close family members)	13	13
37	There has been a serious increase in arguments or problems with someone who lives at home (excluding husband or wife)	16	16
38	There have been serious problems with a close friend, neighbour or relative not living at home	10	8
EDUCATION			
39	You started a course (i.e. University, Tech. College, Business College, apprenticeship or other occupational training course)	3	16
40	You changed to a different course	5	11
41	You completed your training program	2	27
42	You dropped out of your training program	14	22
43	You studied for, or did, important exams	10	13
44	You failed an important exam	20	18
WORK			
45	You have been unemployed and seeking work for a month or more	20	22
46	Your own business failed	38	44
47	You were sacked	32	34
48	You retired	15	53
49	You were downgraded or demoted at work	20	18
50	You were promoted	2	18
51	You began to have trouble or disagreements with your boss, supervisor or fellow workers	10	9
52	You had a big change in the hours you worked	5	16
53	You had a big change in the people, duties or responsibilities in your work	7	17
54	You started in a completely different type of job	8	24
55	You had holidays for a week or more	1	5
MOVING HOUSE			
56	You moved to Australia from overseas	19	48
57	You moved to a new city	8	26
58	You moved house	4	11

	Event	Distress scalings	Life change scalings
FINANCIAL AND LEGAL			
59	You had moderate financial difficulties	9	10
60	You had a major financial crisis	34	37
61	You are much better off financially	1	23
62	You were involved in a traffic accident that carried serious risk to the health or life of yourself or others	31	22
63	You had minor difficulties with the police or the authorities [which has not required a court appearance (e.g. speeding fine, etc)]	4	12
64	You had more important problems with the police or the authorities (leading to a court appearance)	21	15
65	You had a jail sentence or were in prison	59	72
66	You were involved in a civil law suit (e.g. divorce, debt, custody, etc)	25	21
67	Something you valued or cared for greatly was stolen or lost	9	5

Life Events Questionnaire (Andrews)

Scoring:

Where you have marked an event, add the number of points corresponding to the 'Distress' and 'Life Change' scores, respectively.

Interpreting Your Scores:

Distress Scores

	LOW	MEDIUM	HIGH
SCORES	0 to 10	20 to 30	61 to 200

Scores above 61 suggest that you have experienced a significant amount of emotional stress over the past month.

Life Change Scores

	LOW	MEDIUM	HIGH
SCORES	0 to 20	30 to 40	81 to 200

Scores above 81 suggest that your life changes have been exceptionally high recently.

- **Excessive Stress**

Stress can best be understood in terms of mental and physical arousal. Some degree of stress or arousal is a necessary and vital part of life and may provide excitement and challenge. Too little stress for long periods may lead to boredom and loss of self-confidence. For example, after months of unemployment, during periods of illness or while enduring a monotonous job you may lose confidence in your abilities. The less you do, the less you feel like doing. Opportunities for enjoyment become few and far between. At such times you are more susceptible to feeling down.

Helpful Stress Reactions

You may have noticed that you perform better in an exam or a squash match if you are 'charged up' ready for the event. It is important to be aware of how much 'charging up' is necessary for you personally. When we are faced with a danger which may be life-threatening, we need to act quickly. When you are crossing the road, for example, a car may suddenly appear from around the corner, and you need to get out of the way fast. Your body reacts instantly by pumping out adrenalin. When this occurs your heart beats faster, your blood pressure rises, your blood supply is directed to muscles to help you to move, and your breathing rate increases. This is known as the 'flight or fight' response. This response is designed to be a short-term reaction to a serious threat and has great survival value for mankind.

How a Helpful Stress Reaction Becomes Unhelpful

It is not only life or death situations which lead to flight or fight responses. The same response may be triggered by a psychological threat to your well-being, such as fear of job loss or fear of a relationship breakdown. Instead of being a short-term reaction, the fight or flight response may becomc extended over a longer period. When this happens it is common for people to experience anxiety symptoms such as panic attacks and phobias.

Prolonged periods of high anxiety also make you vulnerable to feeling flat afterwards. You may find that you have difficulty making decisions, concentrating or remembering. You may go from one task to another without finishing any of them. If you constantly feel over-stressed and cannot see any way of improving the situation, then feelings of helplessness and hopelessness may develop which lead to the onset of a depression for some people.

The level of stress needed for optimum performance varies from one individual to another. Some people tolerate and thrive on high levels of arousal. It is important for you to determine which level of stress you are comfortable with and adjust your lifestyle accordingly.

• Lifestyle

Over the past few years the media has inundated us with information about the consequences of poor lifestyles on our health. Hearing this so often may make you a little blasé. However, the facts are clear. Stress affects a physically unfit person more than someone who is in good shape.

Looking after your body and ensuring that you have a balanced diet will help minimise stress. Lifestyles that involve skipping meals, overworking and so on, will result in feelings of irritability and depression. The key to a healthy lifestyle is to balance your time across work, leisure, family and other interests so that no one area dominates. This means keeping up your commitments at work but not to the exclusion of your relationships. It also means taking time off to enjoy your hobbies and interests.

Biological Factors

Research has shown that biological depressions tend to run in families. This means that some people are born with greater vulnerability to depression under certain conditions, such as stressful life events.

The three most common biological theories of depression refer to disturbances in the neurotransmitters, hormones and biological rhythms.

Neurotransmitters—these are chemicals which communicate messages between nerve cells in the brain. Low levels of neurotransmitters called noradrenalin and serotonin are particularly associated with depression. Antidepressant medications are thought to work by normalising the function of these chemicals.

Hormones—Abnormalities in hormones have been found in some people suffering from depression. However, mostly the hormonal changes are a consequence of being depressed.

Biological rhythms—Changes found in some depressions appear to be related to disturbances in rhythms from both within and outside us. There is still a lot to learn about how rhythms affect our moods. Some depressed people respond well to being exposed to bright lights which effectively increase their daylight hours.

Therefore seasonal variations in the amount of daylight are thought to affect our moods.

It is becoming increasingly accepted that even when biochemical disturbances are involved in triggering a depression, stress and psychological factors are also involved.

An example of this interplay of several factors is seen in the depression experienced by some women at menopause. The hormonal changes at this time can lead to physical and emotional problems which make women more vulnerable to depression. Not surprisingly, studies show that women who are already having difficulty coping with the stresses of events in middle age are more likely to experience more severe symptoms at menopause.

If you have biochemical disturbances contributing to your depression, then medical treatments can be helpful. There are medications and other physical treatments available which are effective in correcting these disturbances.

Psychological, social and biological factors may contribute to feelings of depression. Each of these needs to be considered when seeking treatment. The chart on p. 26-27 shows the various factors which contributed to David's depression.

Protective Factors

The following coping strategies will protect you from becoming depressed:

1 Building up your self-esteem.

2 Practising positive thinking habits.

3 Expressing your needs, feelings and thoughts assertively.

4 Establishing social supports.

5 Reducing unnecessary stress.

EXERCISE 2 (see p. 28)

You might find it useful now to examine your own personality style.

A number of statements are listed below which relate to how you might feel about yourself and other people in your life. Respond to each statement in terms of how you feel generally, and not necessarily just at present.

Place a number in the box indicating whether each item is—

1 = Very unlike me   3 = Moderately like me

2 = Moderately unlike me   4 = Very like me

	Predisposing factors
SOCIAL FACTORS	*** Social Modelling** Father became depressed at age 50 and started abusing alcohol.
PSYCHOLOGICAL FACTORS	*** Attitudes and Personal Values Leading to Low Self-esteem** **Being a Perfectionist**—'If I'm hard-working and successful, I might avoid failure' **Need for Approval**—'I must do well at work and get my boss's recognition to prove my worth'.
BIOLOGICAL FACTORS	Nil

Triggering factors	Maintaining factors
*** Developmental Crisis** David turned 50 and started reviewing his achievements and his future. *** Taking Responsibility for Son's Developmental Crisis** —Son (age 15) was increasingly irritable and difficult to reason with. *** Stressful Life Event**—Work colleague promoted above David. ***Lifestyle**—Giving up squash. Feeling run down and out of condition.	*** Lack of Confiding Relationships** Continued isolation from family and friends. *** Poor Coping Strategies**—not approaching boss to discuss options and concerns at work.
*** Faulty Thoughts Leading to Depression** 'Everyone at work will know how hopeless I am' 'I'm responsible for my son's behaviour' 'I'm an inadequate father' 'I've let my family down' 'My future is bleak' 'No-one really cares about me. I can't rely on anyone' *** Excessive Stress**—Overworking to prove himself. *** Misattribution of Internal State**—Being overly sensitive to changes in his body and interpreting them as depression, instead of normal irritability or apprehension about his roles at home and work.	***Continued Negative Thinking Maintaining the Depression** 'I'm not going to do anything in case I fail again.' 'This happened to my father—it's genetic. There's nothing I can do about it.'
Nil	Nil

ITEMS

1 I feel insecure when I say goodbye to people [ ]
2 I worry about the effect I have on others [ ]
3 I avoid saying what I think for fear of being ridiculed [ ]
4 I feel uneasy meeting new people [ ]
5 If others knew the real me, they would not like me [ ]
6 I feel secure when I'm in a very close relationship [ ]
7 I don't get angry with people for fear that I may hurt them [ ]
8 After a fight with a friend, I feel uncomfortable until I have made peace [ ]
9 I am always aware of how other people feel [ ]
10 I worry about being criticised for things I have said and done [ ]
11 I always notice if someone doesn't respond to me [ ]
12 I worry about losing someone close to me [ ]
13 I feel that people generally like me [ ]
14 I will do something I don't want to do rather than offend or upset someone [ ]
15 I can only believe that something I have done is good when someone tells me it is [ ]
16 I will go out of my way to please someone I am close to [ ]
17 I feel anxious when I say goodbye to people [ ]
18 I feel happy when someone compliments me [ ]
19 I fear that my feelings will overwhelm people [ ]
20 I can make other people feel happy [ ]
21 I find it hard to get angry with people [ ]
22 I worry about criticising other people [ ]
23 If someone is critical of something I do, I feel bad [ ]
24 If other people knew what I'm really like, they would think less of me [ ]
25 I always expect criticism [ ]
26 I can never be really sure if someone is pleased with me [ ]
27 I don't like people to know me [ ]
28 If someone upsets me, I am not able to put it easily out of my mind [ ]
29 I feel others do not understand me [ ]
30 I worry about what others think of me [ ]
31 I don't feel happy unless people I know admire me [ ]
32 I am never rude to anyone [ ]
33 I worry about hurting the feelings of others [ ]
34 I feel hurt when someone is angry with me [ ]
35 My value as a person depends enormously on what others think of me [ ]
36 I care about what people feel about me [ ]

Interpersonal Sensitivity Measure (IPSM), P. Boyce and G. Parker (1988)

Scoring of the Subscales:

The sub-scale scores are derived by adding your answers on the following items.

Interpersonal Awareness—Items 2, 4, 10, 23, 28, 30, 36
Normal Range: Score 7 - 28

Need for Approval—Items 6, 8, 11, 13, 16, 18, 20, 34
Normal Range: Score 8 - 32

Separation Anxiety—Items 1, 12, 15, 17, 19, 25, 26, 29
Normal Range: Score 8 - 32

Timidity—Items 3, 7, 9, 14, 21, 22, 32, 33
Normal Range: Score 8 - 32

Fragile Inner-self—Items 5, 24, 27, 31, 35
Normal Range: Score 5 - 20

Interpretation of Your Scores

Interpersonal Awareness refers to a sensitivity to interpersonal interactions and what impact you perceive others are having on you. It includes thoughts such as 'I care about what other people feel about me'; 'I worry about the effect I have on other people'. There is also the tendency to worry about the consequences of criticism, for example, 'If someone is critical of what I do, I feel bad'. Scores higher than 19 suggest excessive concern with other people's behaviour in an attempt to gauge their response to you.

Need for Approval describes your need to make others happy and to keep the peace within a relationship. It also involves seeking to ensure that others will like you and not reject you, for instance, 'I will go out of my way to please someone I am close to'. A score higher than 28 suggests subordination of your needs in deference to the wishes of others.

Separation Anxiety measures your attachments to others. Scores higher than 18 suggest that you have an over-sensitivity to any threat of disruption to your bonds with significant others.

Timidity assesses your ability to be assertive in interpersonal situations. Scores higher than 22 suggest that you have difficulty obtaining control over your environment and tend to be non-assertive.

Fragile Inner-self refers to how worthwhile you consider yourself and whether you feel the need to conceal your inner experiences from others. Scores higher than 10 suggest a reluctance to expose your true feelings to others and a fragile self-esteem.

If your scores suggest that it is necessary, you can learn to modify unhelpful attitudes and personality characteristics. You have the choice to adopt an identity in which you see yourself as worthwhile. In doing so, you will be enhancing your coping strategies and protecting yourself against depression.

Chapter 3

HOW YOU THINK YOUR WAY INTO FEELING DOWN

'It is not things in themselves which trouble us, but the opinions we have about these things.'

Epictatus

Cognitive Therapy works by arresting the downward spiral of negative thoughts and reversing the way you feel. If you can think your way into feeling down, then you can certainly think your way into feeling better and more positive.

Two significant principles are involved in Cognitive Therapy:

1 The way you think determines the way you feel.

2 Distortions in thinking play a key role in causing and maintaining distressing feelings.

Thinking habits are developed by life's experiences. This chapter looks at the relationship between thoughts, feelings and behaviour and explains in detail how negative thinking causes unhelpful reactions.

What Causes Our Feelings?

Why would the sight of a baby in a pram cause one woman to become very distressed, another woman to feel completely disinterested and yet another to experience feelings of happiness? The answer lies in the *personal meaning* that each woman associates with the sight of a baby.

Contrary to what you may assume, it is not simply what happens to you that causes your reactions. It is the *meaning* you place on your experiences that leads you to feel and behave in certain ways. This is demonstrated by two important observations.

First, everyone has unique interpretations of particular events based on their personal experiences. These interpretations will determine their emotional reactions. One woman may look at a baby and think 'It's impossible for me to have children'; to another woman, the sight of a child may hold no special significance, while a third woman may be reminded of happy moments with her own child.

Personal meanings cause people to respond differently to the same situation. Hearing a sexist joke may cause some people to laugh, because they find it true and funny. Someone else may react angrily, thinking it is an injustice to women.

Secondly, the same person may react differently to similar events on different occasions. You may have noticed this yourself. Sometimes you may feel irritable when someone teases you, yet at other times you may laugh with them. Your stream of thoughts or images *at the time* of the event is what determines how you will react. If the interpretation you make when someone teases you is something like 'she's putting me down', you are most likely to become annoyed. At another time you may think, 'she's in a playful mood, I'll play along'.

Belief Systems

Belief systems are the way you have learnt to view your world, your experiences and yourself. The meaning you place on an event, the significance the event has to you and the imagery it evokes is determined by your belief system.

Your beliefs and personal values are formed by early childhood experiences. These beliefs are either confirmed or modified by further experiences you have throughout your life. Beliefs form the basis of your personal philosophy towards life and will influence how you react in various situations. A few examples of belief systems are:

Do unto others as you would have them do unto you.

Everyone gets what they deserve.

Everything has a purpose.

Belief systems can be negative, 'I have no control over what happens to me', or positive, 'the world is basically a good place'. Without you necessarily being aware of it, these beliefs cause you to tune into certain information or experiences and to screen out others. The person who believes he has little control over what happens,

I DON'T AMOUNT TO A HILL OF BEANS...
I NEVER BRING HOME THE BACON...
I ALWAYS END UP WITH EGG ON MY FACE...
...AND I ACT THE SILLY SAUSAGE.
I'M A REAL BREAKFAST CASE.

is most likely to focus on and recall instances that confirm this belief. On the other hand, the person with the more positive attitude will tune into positive experiences and tend to dismiss the unpleasant ones. This is how biases in thinking occur.

This process of tuning into or screening out certain information is called filtering and is demonstrated by the following example.

An empty bus leaves the depot for the day's run. On the first stop, it picks up 10 people . . . next stop it picks up 20 people . . . then it lets off 15 people at the next stop . . . after this 30 people are picked up . . . then it lets off 20 people . . . next it picks up 40. The question is, how many stops did the bus make?

This example shows how a bias may have occurred in your thinking. You probably assumed that one set of information, namely the number of passengers, is more important than the other information received, namely the number of stops. You were also probably unaware of this bias in the way you gave attention to certain facts and disregarded others.

As well as influencing how you select information, your biases also affect the way in which you understand or explain your experiences. Consider the following example:

A little boy was wheeled into the emergency room of a hospital. The surgeon came in to examine the child and exclaimed in surprise, 'son!'. But the surgeon was not the boy's father.

If you assume that all surgeons are male, you would have difficulty solving this puzzle. The surgeon is of course the boy's mother.

Belief systems can cause biases and assumptions to be made as you try to understand your life experiences. You are not necessarily aware when such biases or assumptions are operating. Nor do you need to challenge them, unless they spoil the quality of your life. For example, a person may believe that he is inferior to others. This belief may be confirmed because it causes a bias to dwell on only negative things about himself and filter out any positives. As a result, he thinks his belief is reasonable.

Your everyday thoughts and images give important clues about which beliefs cause biases and so affect your behaviour and moods in unhelpful ways. These everday thoughts and images, known as automatic thoughts, are described later in this chapter.

Helpful beliefs allow for flexibility in your judgements of things and for the possibility that both you and the others might be wrong on occasions. They help you to respect yourself and maintain your self-esteem.

The ABC of Thinking, Feeling and Behaving

It is not the event itself, but rather how you interpret it at that particular moment, that determines how you feel.

This process is illustrated by the following diagram:

A EVENTS (imagined or real)

↓

B THOUGHTS

↓

C REACTIONS (feelings and behaviour)

Imagine that you are standing up on a bus and someone bumps into you from behind resulting in you plunging into the lap of an unsuspecting passenger. Your immediate reaction may be one of anger provoked by thoughts such as:

> What a fool. He should be more careful. I shouldn't have to put up with this.

The reality of that moment, as you see it, is that you have been mistreated. If you then discover that the person who bumped you is blind, your feelings may alter. The situation is the same, but your perceptions and interpretations have changed. Your attitude towards blind people will probably allow you to be more sympathetic and reduce your anger at being pushed.

A Events are situations which you react to, such as being criticised by your partner, not finding what you are looking for, being asked by your boss to do extra work, or meeting an old friend.

Imagined events can lead to the same reactions as real events. If you believe something to be true, you will react as though it were true. Your thoughts alone trigger emotional and physical reactions just as if the event had really occurred. The following example illustrates this.

David's wife did not call to say that she would be late home. As time passed the thought came to him that she could be having an affair. Once this suspicion took hold of him, he began to believe that it was true. He felt hurt, rejected and angry and even started planning in his mind how he was going to retaliate. When his wife arrived home, she told how she had been held up in a traffic jam caused by a serious car accident. David's wife could not understand why he was so upset and angry with her for being late.

B Thoughts are based on personal values and beliefs which you have learnt over time. To become more aware of the meanings you give to events you need to pay close attention to your thinking at the time you became upset. By noticing what you are saying to yourself you will be able to identify particular beliefs that cause unhelpful reactions.

C Reactions are your responses to your thoughts and consist of feelings and behaviour.

- **Feelings** are fundamental to our existence as human beings. Without them we would be boring, bored and mechanical. Feelings are not spontaneous, but arise as a result of the personal meanings given to our experiences. Two salesmen, waiting for an important client who is late for a business luncheon, react according to their individual interpretations. One sees the client's lateness as a sign of disinterest and becomes anxious thinking he will lose the sale. The other stays relaxed, assuming that the client is merely busy and has been inadvertently delayed.

We often give different labels to feelings depending on their strength. When feelings become intense, it is more difficult, if not impossible, to stay in control of a situation. You may react in ways that you later regret. The scale below shows how feelings are labelled as they develop in intensity from 0-100%

0%	50%	100%
indifferent	annoyed disappointed concerned	enraged depressed panicked

- **Behaviour**, too, is affected by how events are interpreted. The anxiety experienced by the salesman may cause him to behave less confidently towards his client. Alternatively, he may behave more aggressively to ensure that the sale is made.

How You Can Tell if You Are Overreacting

Feelings can be assessed according to how helpful they are. Helpful emotional reactions enable you to achieve goals, deal with the stresses of everyday or major problems and feel in control. Unhelpful emotional reactions, on the other hand, interfere with your functioning and stop you from dealing effectively with problems.

In deciding what shape your emotions are in, you need to consider the following factors:

- how long the feeling lasts for
- how severe the feeling is in relation to the triggering event
- how often you feel this way
- whether your emotions are having a helpful effect on your life and plans.

The duration of your reaction will depend on the severity of the event you are confronted with. There are of course many individual differences in how long people take to get over things. Emotional overreactions occur when the reaction by far outlasts the significance of the triggering event. One man described how he used to get worked up when caught in morning peak hour traffic jams and this affected his mood for the rest of the day.

The intensity of your feelings is usually strongest during and soon after the event and should ease with time. If the intensity has not reduced over time, this suggests that adequate re-adjustment has not occurred. Some people we have seen in therapy show persistent and intense emotions associated with events that happened five, ten and even twenty years ago. Feelings harboured over such a long time are unhelpful and may disrupt current relationships and functioning.

The frequency with which you experience certain feelings can also indicate whether emotional problems exist. If you commonly experience annoyance or depression in response to everyday situations, it probably means that you are overreacting. If you repeatedly feel upset when dealing with a particular person or situation, this indicates that a change in your reactions is required.

Emotional *underreactions* can also be unhelpful. If there is a valid reason to be upset or angry and you do not express these feelings, anxiety and depression can result. Underreacting usually occurs when you lack self-confidence or assertion skills.

Emotions are internal monitoring systems giving feedback about your progress towards goals. Positive emotions such as excitement and pleasure are signs that you are pleased with your progress. Unpleasant emotions such as frustration or disappointment are signs to reassess your behaviour and your goals. If you use unpleasant feelings to make changes in yourself or your environment, then they have been helpful. If you see unpleasant emotions as major setbacks and you allow them to stop you achieving goals, they are clearly unhelpful.

Automatic Thoughts or Thinking Habits

The term automatic thoughts refers to the images, daydreams, fantasies and train of thoughts that go through your mind in response to everyday situations. These thoughts appear to arise by reflex, without prior reflection or reasoning. This happens because we generally pay little attention to the way we think and so do not notice when a particular thought or image becomes a habit.

When something becomes a habit, you behave automatically. The advantage in being able to react automatically is that you are able to do things more quickly, you have time to think about creative things and to plan what you will do next. The disadvantage is that you have less control over your feelings and behaviours.

The secretary, who automatically said 'of course' to her boss's request to work late, found herself becoming more and more irritated as the afternoon progressed. Her automatic thought that she should do as the boss requested, conflicted with her wish to watch a favourite movie on television. Her annoyance set off a further stream of automatic thoughts along these lines: 'He's just using me. He didn't even ask if I had anything planned for tonight. He's taking advantage of my good nature'. By the time she arrived home, she was in such a bad mood, she was unable to enjoy the remainder of the movie.

Because automatic thoughts occur spontaneously and naturally, you may not realise that they are simply your interpretations and not facts. Automatic thoughts seem more believable because the ideas are so familiar. The more often you say something to yourself, the more likely it is that you will believe it. Automatic thoughts are like a well worn, comfortable pair of shoes which are secure and familiar in the way they slip on. Because of this familiarity, new ways of interpreting events will often seem unbelievable. New thoughts, like new shoes, need to be worn in if they are to feel like yours.

You may forget that other people view things differently. For instance, you may feel quite offended or hurt if friends forget your birthday, not realising that they don't fuss over anyone's birthday—not even their own. You can't assume that other people automatically understand how and why you feel the way you do.

Automatic thoughts are learned habits which can be changed if necessary. With a bit of effort, you can become aware of your automatic thoughts.

Types of Automatic Thoughts

Automatic thoughts may be neutral, positive or negative.

Neutral thoughts—are those in which no evaluation is made and the topic is usually non-emotional, for example, 'my keys are on the bench'.

Positive thoughts—increase the likelihood that you will either achieve the goal you have set yourself, or that you will feel good. For example, 'It may be difficult mixing with people at the party tonight, but I'll give it a go'. Positive thoughts need to be logical and realistic. As a result, your subsequent feelings are less intense and more easily controlled. This in turn enables you to be more effective in dealing with any difficulties that may arise.

Negative thoughts—can prevent you from achieving your goal because they are self-critical, which inevitably reduces your self-confidence.

When Do Automatic Thoughts Become a Problem?

Thinking habits only become a problem if you find yourself frequently feeling down or easily upset and your feelings are interfering with your ability to handle effectively everyday or major stresses.

Automatic thoughts can become a problem if they prevent you from learning or trying alternative ways of coping with stress. The person who thinks 'It's no use, I'll never get them to accept my idea', or, 'I can't do anything about this', blocks himself from exploring alternatives.

If you tell yourself often enough that you cannot cope, then you will end up believing it and so stop yourself from learning new ways of coping.

You may be able to think of some of your own negative thoughts. Do you have regular put-downs such as:

I'm hopeless at such and such.
No one could be as unhappy as I am.
I can't cope—it's all too much.

Identifying Your Automatic Thoughts

If you feel you have little control over your feelings, it is important that you examine the way you are thinking. If you repeatedly have intense feelings such as depression, anxiety or anger, this suggests that you need to change some of your automatic thoughts. You can identify thoughts which may contribute to your depression by completing Exercise 4.

EXERCISE 4

Listed below are a variety of thoughts that pop into people's heads. Read each thought and indicate how frequently, if at all, the thought occurred to you *over the last week*. Please read each item carefully and rate it on a scale 1 to 5 where 1 = NOT AT ALL, 2 = SOMETIMES, 3 = MODERATELY OFTEN, 4 = OFTEN, 5 = ALL THE TIME.

I feel like I"m up against the world.	☐
I'm no good.	☐
Why can't I ever succeed?	☐
No one understands me.	☐
I've let people down.	☐
I don't think I can go on.	☐
I wish I were a better person.	☐
I'm so weak.	☐
My life's not going the way I want it to.	☐
I'm so disappointed in myself.	☐
Nothing feels good anymore.	☐

I can't stand this anymore.	☐
I can't get started.	☐
What's wrong with me?	☐
I wish I were somewhere else.	☐
I can't get things together.	☐
I hate myself.	☐
I'm worthless.	☐
Wish I could just disappear.	☐
What's the matter with me?	☐
I'm a loser.	☐
My life is a mess.	☐
I'm a failure.	☐
I'll never make it.	☐
I feel so helpless.	☐
Something has to change.	☐
There must be something wrong with me.	☐
My future is bleak.	☐
It's just not worth it.	☐
I can't finish anything.	☐

The Automatic Thoughts Questionnaire (Hollon and Kendall)

Now add up your score to calculate your current total of automatic thoughts. The more severe your depression, the higher your score will be. The maximum score is 150 and the minimum is 30.

After using the techniques in this book for about four weeks, complete the questionnaire again and compare scores. Some of the people we have treated have found that their scores dropped by as much as 100 points over a four week period. You may also be pleasantly surprised!

What Causes Distressing and Uncontrollable Feelings?

Our clinical experience has convinced us that illogical and distorted thinking play key roles in causing and maintaining distressing feelings. Exaggerated thinking and negative assumptions lead to emotional overreactions.

This is shown by Katherine's reaction to an incident when her husband was caught up in a work meeting and was hours late for dinner. Katherine made many negative assumptions such as, 'He doesn't care, he doesn't appreciate the effort I make for his meals, he can't even be bothered to phone me'. When he arrived home, stressed and tired from the meeting, she attacked him with these accusations. Because she believed her negative assumptions, Katherine did not accept her husband's apology.

If your thinking is logical, your feelings will be less intense, more controllable and more realistic. As a result, your behaviour is more effective in dealing with problems.

Thinking Patterns in Depression

Aaron Beck has described three important aspects of negative thinking experienced by people who are feeling depressed.

1 A Negative View of Yourself

I'm not good enough.
Why can't I be like everyone else?
I'm a failure.

When feeling depressed you tend to view yourself in a highly critical and self-blaming way. Aaron Beck proposes that depressed people set unrealistically high goals that cannot be achieved and so a sense of failure results. You may feel inadequate or inferior to others and believe that you have deficiencies which you cannot overcome. You may regard yourself as undesirable and worthless, and believe that you lack attributes essential for happiness. When depressed, you focus on your shortcomings and ignore your positive points. This is the filtering process we described earlier in this chapter.

When you are depressed, you tend to blame yourself for situations that did not turn out well. Depressed people blame themselves if things do not work out, but will not give themselves credit if things do work out! In fact, they view their success as due to good luck rather than due to anything they have done! If you think this way, you will not build up your self-esteem or self-confidence, but will continue to feel rather helpless and ineffective. This shows a bias in how you understand or explain your experiences.

2 A Negative View of Your Experiences

When depressed, it is common to feel helpless about changing your situation. It may seem that insurmountable obstacles are constantly preventing you from reaching your goals. There is also a tendency to misinterpret past and present experiences and to focus on things which you believe prove your feelings of defeat. You may be overly sensitive to criticism and rejection. By screening out the positive things in your life, you develop a very biased picture.

3 A Negative View of the Future

If you expect that unpleasant experiences are highly likely to happen to you, and that you can do nothing to change this, feelings of helplessness and lack of control will follow. For instance,

It's hopeless.
I'll never get over this.
Things will always be the same for me.

You may anticipate that your problems will continue indefinitely and that you will always feel bad. You will expect continued hardship, frustration and failure and dwell on all the worst things that could happen to you and your loved ones.

How Unpleasant Feelings Can Be Motivators to Change

Feelings such as dissatisfaction, disappointment or annoyance tell you that change is necessary. For instance, if you are feeling frustrated by the boring routine of your job, you are more likely to do something about it.

Positive thinking encourages you to use an unpleasant feeling as a motivation for action and change. How productively you are able to use unpleasant emotions is dependent on your thinking style. People who cope well with life stresses are those who are able to turn negative experiences into positive ones. The secret lies in your thinking.

Change Your Feelings by Changing Your Thinking

If your thinking habits are negative and illogical, you will most likely view situations in ways that will leave you feeling down. Accepting that the way you view things has become a habit puts you in a powerful position to change your thinking so that you may control your reactions. By challenging negative thoughts, you can develop a thinking style which is more helpful in dealing with problems and reducing intense, unpleasant feelings.

A constructive thinking style acknowledges difficulties and enables you to deal with them more effectively. Consider the following example:

SITUATION ↓	Increasing arguments ↓
NEGATIVE THOUGHTS ↓	We do not get on at all anymore. If this relationship breaks up I'll have no one and I'll be horribly lonely. I can't cope going on like this. ↓
REACTIONS, FEELINGS, BEHAVIOUR	Anxiety, depression and loss of confidence. Increasing dependency on partner.

Here is an alternative way of handling the same event following a change in thinking style:

SITUATION	Increasing arguments. ↓
POSITIVE THOUGHTS	We could do something to resolve our problems. I want to improve this relationship if I can. I will try to talk about our problems. Maybe we could try professional counselling. ↓
REACTIONS, FEELINGS,	Some anxiety but also some hope. ↓
BEHAVIOUR	Seeking help, focusing on positives and improving relationship.

Learning to Think Realistically

Constructive thinking is not simply looking through rose-coloured glasses and bluffing yourself that you do not have a problem. For instance, the interviewee will not be helping himself by thinking, 'This interview will be a breeze. There is no way that I will miss out on the job'.

False positive thoughts can be as unrealistic as negative thoughts, and leave you feeling just as bad. Examples of false positive messages might include:

I'll be positive and confident no matter what.
If I do this, I'll never get depressed again.

False positive thoughts set up unrealistic expectations which will lead to a feeling of failure and hopelessness if things do not work out. They also block you from planning effectively and resolving problems.

A constructive and realistic thinking style acknowledges problems and explores ways of overcoming them. For example, the realistic interviewee would say to himself, 'I may get a bit nervous in the interview, but that's OK. I've done some preparation and will try to do my best'.

Breaking the Habit

The techniques in this book help you to become more aware of your negative automatic thoughts and how they contribute to your depression or other intense, uncontrolled feelings. Later chapters outline specific styles of thinking that are illogical and distorted and thus lead to emotional overreactions, depression and anxiety. In order to change your thinking so you have more control over your emotions, it is necessary for you to identify and challenge faulty thinking habits. The more time that you put into it, the sooner you will experience the benefits.

The techniques in the next few chapters will help you to exchange a more productive thinking habit for your old one.

Common Negative Thoughts About Depression

Listed below are some negative automatic thoughts which people often have. If you share any of them, you may find it useful to study the corresponding constructive responses.

Negative thoughts	Positive responses
I must not admit that I'm depressed	It is important to recognise and acknowledge my depression so that I can do something about it.
Others are getting me down.	My negative thinking is getting me down. I will take responsibility for my emotions.
My life was perfect once, why can't things go back to how they were?	Maybe I'm idealising the past. I'll try to make the most of the future.
Everyone is happier and more confident than I am.	I don't really know this. I will think about what I can do to help myself feel better and not worry about everyone else.
I need someone stronger than I am. I can't cope alone.	I will learn about my capabilities by taking on as much as I can without depending on others.
I am a sensitive person so I feel things more intensely than others.	I can control my sensitivity through my thinking. I don't have to react so intensely to situations if I don't want to.
If only someone could understand how I feel.	Having others understand may not necessarily make me feel better. I can work on feeling better irrespective of the reactions of others.
I must be a weak person to get depressed.	Just because I'm feeling down doesn't mean that I'm a weak person. No one operates at 100% all the time.
The depression has harmed me permanently—mentally and physically.	Feelings are not permanent, but transitory experiences. My abilities will return when I'm feeling better.

Negative thoughts	Positive responses
There is no point. I can't change the situation.	I will make an effort to change what I don't like and accept what I can't change. At least I can change my attitudes.
I can't feel any better because I have too many problems.	I will take one day at a time and set daily goals for myself. I will allow myself time to get over this.
My future wili always be bleak.	I will make some practical plans to improve things in the future.
Why me? It's not fair that I should be down.	I might be experiencing difficulties now, but everyone has problems from time to time.
No one can help me.	There is no reason to believe that other people won't be helpful in certain ways. Only by asking them will I find out if and how they can help.
It's up to others to make me feel better.	Other people can help in some ways and guide me but ultimately it is up to me.
Someone, somewhere knows all the answers and will tell me the solution.	There is no solution or magic wand that can cure all my problems. Getting better involves effort over a period of time.
There is no point in trying. I've tried things before and they didn't help.	I won't know if this technique will help unless I try.

Over to Michelle who will tell you how she went about challenging her negative thoughts:

I was asked to write something for this book because I was good at identifying my negative automatic thoughts. Well as soon as it was stated that I was good at it, my mind went into a spin!

I'll make a mess of it. I'll let Jill and Sue down.
I won't be able to do what is wanted.

Of course all this made me feel very down, rather anxious and my mind was so busy being negative that I failed to take note of what I was supposed to be doing. My rising anxiety was stopping me from putting my ideas down and was, in turn, making me feel more depressed!

How could I have handled it differently?

I could have said thank you for the compliment and then asked questions to clarify what was required. I could have told myself that it would be good to be able to help others as I had been helped. If what I write doesn't fit into the book, I'll still be able to practise the skills.

Well, here is my story. I am now 28 years of age and have suffered from depressive episodes since my early teenage years. At this time

I was angry with my parents, especially my father, who set expectations which I could never seem to reach. I desperately wanted their approval and only seemed to get affection when I was ill.

I started a Science Degree at University, but this was interrupted by a serious breakdown, during which time I became suicidal and lost all interest in life. After the blackness had lifted my confidence was low. I did voluntary work for a while before returning to study. For the past six years I have been working as a teacher. I live alone and have some friends but do not let them get too close to me. I had a relationship for some time but this did not work out and we have since gone our separate ways.

Here are some of my old thinking habits:	Here are the positive realisations I am coming to:
I can't get away from my past. I'm scarred for life.	The past cannot be changed but I can stop it afflicting my future. I don't have to be a victim of my past if I don't want to.
If people really knew me they wouldn't like me.	We all have parts of us or behaviours that we don't like and there are lots of things about us that are likeable.
I desperately try to get everyone's approval but no one likes me.	Not everyone will like me and I won't like everyone else either. In actual fact I do have some friends and could get closer to them if I wanted to.
It would be best if I stayed away from people because I'm no good at relationships.	If I stay away from people I don't give myself a chance to get to first base in forming a relationship. I'd probably be all right if I just relaxed and tried to enjoy the other person's company.
I need to belong to someone in order to be happy.	No one belongs to anyone. People have relationships at various times in their lives. It is OK not to be in an intimate relationship.
It is the worst thing in the world to fail.	I can't be good at everything that I do. It's important to give things a go. It is not useful or logical to see everything in terms of success or failure.
It is wrong to think well of myself.	If I don't like myself how can I expect anyone else to like me, or for me to like anyone else.

I have had drug treatment and psychotherapy of various sorts with numerous therapists. They probably helped me in some way because I am still alive. But my happiness was always dependent on something or someone else.

Cognitive Therapy put the onus for improvement back in my own hands. For me this is good because there is something that I can do for myself. Just knowing that there is something that I can do when I am down is very helpful. I am now starting to believe in myself a bit more and I am planning for my future for the first time. I've realised that I do deserve a future.

Monitoring Your Moods

It is important that you now start to become more aware of the relationship between the thoughts, feelings and events in your everyday life. You can use the daily recording form to help with this. By recording what you were doing and thinking at the time you felt down, you will be able to obtain useful information about the causes of your moods. Start now and continue to fill out the daily recording form each day for the next two or three weeks.

Depression
Daily Recording Form

DAY ____________ DATE ____________

Today, on average my mood was:

Circle one number: 1 2 3 4 5 6 7 8 9

Low Medium Really great

Today, my *worst* mood was: Time: ____________

What were you doing? ____________

What were you thinking about? ____________

Circle one number to indicate your mood at the time:

1 2 3 4 5 6 7 8 9

Low Medium Really great

Today, my *best* mood was: Time: ____________

What were you doing? ____________

What were you thinking about? ____________

Circle one number to indicate your mood at the time:

1 2 3 4 5 6 7 8 9

Low Medium Really great

Daily Mood Monitoring Form (Wilson, Spence and Kavanagh)

Chapter 4

BREAKING THE LETHARGY CIRCUIT

> *'Habit is habit and is not to be flung out the window, but to be coaxed downstairs a step at a time.'*
>
> *MARK TWAIN*

There are two main ways of mastering your moods. The first focuses on changes in your thinking. The second involves changes in what you do.

When feeling down, you may lose interest in doing things. Activities which used to give you pleasure may no longer do so. Perhaps your lifestyle has changed and you no longer have the opportunity to enjoy things as you used to. This may happen after an illness, accident, separation from your partner, and so on.

When depressed, you may find it difficult to get on with basic daily tasks. If you are suffering from fatigue or poor concentration, then you will probably find yourself becoming less and less active. David talks about his feelings of lethargy:

> As soon as I wake up in the morning, the routine tasks of getting out of bed, washing, eating, even brushing my teeth seem to require herculean effort. As I face the day all I can see is a series of hurdles to overcome. Thinking about these tasks saps the energy and enthusiasm from my body. My thoughts and actions slow down. I cannot concentrate and I am easily confused. If I find the energy to carry out a task I feel that the job is never done well enough or fast enough. I cannot trust myself to make decisions so I procrastinate endlessly about each task to be done.

Lack of Motivation

Many people are enthusiastic and energetic when they are not feeling down. However, when depressed, their motivation to do things disappears and procrastination sets in. What is happening is that negative thoughts are serving as activity blocks. You may recognise some of the following in your own thinking:

Everything is too difficult. I can't even do simple things anymore.
I'm not in the mood to do anything.
I can't be bothered.
I must do things as well as I used to.
I feel too anxious (or depressed) to be able to enjoy myself.
There is no point. I don't have the energy and besides, I will only fail.

When you are not doing very much, you tend to believe that you are ineffective, inadequate, helpless and incapable of achieving anything. These negative thoughts will make you feel more discouraged, and in turn further reduce your ability to be active. If this continues, it becomes even more difficult to get to work, to get jobs done around the house and to get on with your usual activities. You may spend more time alone and avoid situations. Consequently, there are fewer opportunities for you to obtain pleasure and a sense of achievement. This whole process sets off a vicious cycle which keeps you feeling down. It has been called the lethargy circuit.[1]

The Lethargy Circuit

You can see how the lethargy circuit works from the following diagram.

NEGATIVE THOUGHTS (OR ACTIVITY BLOCKS)
'There is no point in trying.'

↓

SELF-DEFEATING FEELINGS
Feeling discouraged, inadequate and helpless

↓

SELF-DEFEATING ACTIONS
Avoiding situations

Here is the lethargy circuit in action:

Situation 1 Michelle had been feeling down for some months. Her local doctor suggested that she enrol in the Cognitive Therapy Group.

Michelle's Negative Thoughts

If my doctor really understood how depressed I am, he wouldn't expect me to do something like this.
He's probably given up on me because he thinks I'm a hopeless case.
There is no point in going to the group. I'm too depressed and wouldn't be able to handle it.
It would make me anxious and I couldn't cope with that as well. It would make me feel worse. I couldn't face anyone anyhow. I'm not in the mood.
I'd probably say something stupid, because I can't think clearly. Everyone would think I'm a fool. It would be a waste of time.

↓

SELF-DEFEATING FEELINGS

Michelle then felt even more discouraged, helpless and guilty. Her thoughts also led to feelings of anger and rejection.

↓

SELF-DEFEATING ACTIONS

Michelle didn't get to the Cognitive Therapy Group. Instead she chose to stay in bed and avoided friends and family.

↓

CONSEQUENCES

Michelle believed this incident proved that she really was a failure. She tended to become even more depressed and isolated, which in turn led to further self-defeating thoughts.

When you are upset, you may allow your feelings to guide the way you act. For instance, if you feel useless, you may convince yourself that there is no point in trying. As a result, you will tend to withdraw, avoid situations and reduce your level of activity. You are doing this because you have let your unpleasant feelings decide what you should do.

The trick is to realise that your feelings are not necessarily valid. They often have little bearing on the truth. Your feelings of being too depressed to cope do not mean that you will be unable to cope when you are actually in the situation. Many people cope much better than they anticipated.

Situation 2 Three weeks later, Michelle was not feeling any better. Her therapist helped her to challenge some of her negative thoughts. He again suggested that she enrol in the Cognitive Therapy Group. These are Michelle's modified thoughts which encouraged her to attend the sessions:

Michelle's Positive Thoughts

Lying in bed doesn't seem to have helped me.
Going to the group may be difficult, but I've got nothing to lose.
I'll consider it as an experiment. If it helps that's good, if not, at least I've tried.
The group is for people with depression, so they may understand how difficult it is for me to get there and participate.
Unless I try, I won't know if it will be helpful or not.
Just making the effort is a significant achievement, given the way that I'm feeling.

↓

FEELINGS

Although she felt anxious about trying something new, Michelle also felt more prepared to take on a challenge.

↓

ACTIONS

Michelle arrived at the group and was surprised to find that it was easier than she had expected. She was also relieved to meet other people who were trying to get on top of their depression.

↓

CONSEQUENCES

Each week Michelle took on a little more and she gradually started to feel better about herself. She also discovered that it is often necessary to put up with some anxiety or emotional discomfort in order to feel better in the long term. Had Michelle kept listening to her depressive thoughts, she would not have given herself the opportunity to feel better.

Do the Opposite to What Your Depression Tells You To Do

If you are inclined to stay in bed, then get out. If you do not want to go to the concert, then go. It is important not to let your down moods take control and guide the way you act.

Staying Active When Feeling Down

There are many sound reasons for staying active when you are feeling down:

- The more you do, the more you feel like doing. The less you do, the less you want to do.
- Your motivation will improve by having tackled something. There is a chain reaction effect. Everything you do when feeling down is likely to motivate you to attempt something else.
- Activities are often a source of enjoyment or achievement. Participation in them may make you feel better.
- Negative thoughts are based on assumptions. Avoiding activities does not give you the opportunity to check out whether your negative thoughts are true or not. Attempting tasks establishes what you can and cannot do.
- By becoming involved in an activity, you are more likely to give yourself a break from negative thoughts. Many people notice that when left alone their thinking automatically focuses on something distressing. By trying to concentrate on something else, you may be able to distract yourself from unhelpful thoughts, even if only for a brief period.
- Self-confidence is improved by having a go at something and then putting in some practice to improve your performance.

Avoiding activities only makes you feel worse about yourself.

- There is a physical reason for being active when you are feeling down. If you confine yourself to your bed or house each day, you will experience a lack of stimulation. This leads to changes in your nervous system which cause further emotional distress. For this reason, you should get out of the house for a while each day. You may choose to go into your garden, walk around the block, visit a neighbour or sit in the park. You need daily input and some stimulation from your environment in order to feel good emotionally.

Getting More Out of Your Day

Step 1 Gradually increase the amount of things that you do by planning specific activities each day. This gives you more control over what happens and provides more opportunities for enjoyment and achievement. Planning specific activities in a detailed way helps you to pace your day and lessens the tendency to slip back into passivity and negative thinking. Use the activity plan as your guide.[2]

Step 2 Rate the degree of pleasure (P) and achievement (A) which you experience from each activity. Rate your activities from 0 to 5 (after completing them) on the following scale.

The Pleasure Scale (P) refers to the feelings of enjoyment which you get from the activity. By increasing your opportunities for pleasurable experiences you can make yourself feel better. Maintaining a reasonable degree of pleasure can also help prevent you from becoming depressed again.

0——1——2——3——4——5

NO PLEASURE	SOME PLEASURE	MAXIMUM PLEASURE

The Achievement Scale (A) refers to the sense of accomplishment or achievement gained from having taken on the activity. Achievement is affected by how difficult the task was for you at that time. If the activity is a difficult one for you right now and you attempt it, then you give yourself a high Achievement (A) rating. For instance, getting yourself off to work when not depressed may not seem like a very difficult task. When down, it may be an ordeal. Cooking, going to the bank, or seeing friends may all be high achievement tasks when you are feeling down.

0——1——2——3——4——5

NO ACHIEVEMENT	SOME ACHIEVEMENT	MAXIMUM ACHIEVEMENT

Instructions for Using the Activity Plan

1 Plan one day at a time.

2 Plan the activities the night before for the following day.

3 Plan activities on an hour to hour basis.

4 Break tasks into small steps.

5 Plan to include some activities which usually give you pleasure and also include some increasingly difficult tasks.

6 Work towards getting back to the routine you had before you were depressed and include activities which you used to enjoy.

7 Keep to the activity plan as closely as possible. However, you will also need to be flexible.

8 If an activity is missed, just proceed with the next one.

9 Record your Pleasure (P) and Achievement (A) ratings for each activity, as soon as possible after the event. The ratings between 0 and 5 refer to how you were feeling during the activity.

10 Note any additional activities that occurred during the day and record their P and A ratings.

11 Try the Activity Plan for at least a week. If possible, continue until you have resumed your usual routine.

12 If you know that certain activities tend to make you tense, then plan to do some relaxation exercises immediately beforehand.

The Activity Plan

Katherine found that she felt down when alone in the house after her children had gone to school. Here is her Activity Plan.

Date: Monday

Hours	Activity	Ratings (P)	(A)
7-8 AM	Get up and dressed	P 0	A 3
8-9 AM	Breakfast	P 0	A 1
9-10 AM	Hand wash one item of clothing	P 0	A 3
10-11 AM	Read headlines in the newspaper	P 2	A 2
11-12 AM	Relaxation tape	P 3	A 2
12-1 PM	Lunch with friend	P 3	A 3
1-2 PM	Walk to local shop	P 0	A 0
2-3 PM	Sit in park	P 1	A 1
3-4 PM	Talk with children	P 5	A 0
4-5 PM	Make some phone calls	P 2	A 5
5-6 PM	Cook meal	P 0	A 1
6-7 PM	Dinner with family	P 3	A 1
7-8 PM	Watch TV	P 1	A 0
8-9 PM	Soak in bath	P 5	A 0
9-12 PM	Read a magazine in bed	P 2	A 1

Getting Started

If you find the activity plan difficult, build up to it gradually. Try setting just one pleasure and one achievement activity for each day. This will help you to get started. Next build up to two pleasure and two achievement activities, remembering to work at one easily obtainable goal first.

If you have trouble getting going, it may be necessary to use some self-encouraging messages to talk yourself into doing the task:

I won't know what it will be like until I try.
Sitting here is only making me feel worse, I've got nothing to lose.
It will probably get easier once I have started.
Last time I did feel better afterwards, so it is worth trying again.
I know I usually enjoy this when I'm feeling good, so I'll give it a go.

Gathering Evidence—Are Things Really As Bad As I Think?

Collecting information which tests the validity of your negative thoughts is a helpful step in overcoming the blues. The fact that you are down suggests that you believe your thoughts to be true.

The activity plan can help you dispute your thoughts.

For example, Katherine was becoming increasingly irritable and withdrawn. She identified the following negative thoughts:

> Because I get no enjoyment from being with people anymore, I'm better off alone.

By using the Activity Plan, it became evident to Katherine that she did in fact get some enjoyment from being with her children and friends. The other piece of interesting information was that she had lower pleasure ratings on activities when she was alone than when she made the effort to be with these people. She discovered that her negative belief was incorrect.

Up and Running

A periodic review of your activity plan and your pattern of pleasure and achievement ratings helps you to build on successes and put less emphasis on problems. As you identify activities which give you pleasure, continue to include them in your day and look for other activities you might also enjoy. In doing so you are gaining control of your time, your feelings, and your life. You will no longer be the passive victim of your negative thoughts.

The following list may give you some ideas for pleasurable activities. The activities range from everyday walks, to more adventurous pursuits such as rock climbing. Tailor the activities to your needs and interests.

EXERCISE 6

List of Pleasant Events

Instructions: Place a tick in the first column indicating which activities you would like to pursue over the next few days. Place a tick in the second column indicating which activities you would be prepared to pursue over the next few months.

	Next few days	Next few months
Social Activities		
Being with someone you like	[ ]	[ ]
Writing a letter	[ ]	[ ]
Telephoning a friend	[ ]	[ ]

	Next few days	Next few months
Visiting someone	[ ]	[ ]
Doing something for someone you like	[ ]	[ ]
Inviting a friend around	[ ]	[ ]
Having lunch in a cafe	[ ]	[ ]
Going out for a social drink	[ ]	[ ]
Going to a restaurant	[ ]	[ ]
Going to a dinner party	[ ]	[ ]
Giving a dinner party	[ ]	[ ]
Having a picnic or barbeque	[ ]	[ ]
Asking for a cuddle	[ ]	[ ]
Enjoying an intimate time with someone you care about	[ ]	[ ]
Joining a club related to your interests, politics or sport	[ ]	[ ]
Church activities	[ ]	[ ]
Dancing	[ ]	[ ]
Being with children	[ ]	[ ]
Playing cards or Trivial Pursuit	[ ]	[ ]
Creative Activities		
Art	[ ]	[ ]
Pottery	[ ]	[ ]
Photography	[ ]	[ ]
Drama	[ ]	[ ]
Writing poetry or prose	[ ]	[ ]
Playing a musical instrument	[ ]	[ ]
Singing	[ ]	[ ]
Cooking	[ ]	[ ]
Knitting	[ ]	[ ]
Sewing	[ ]	[ ]
Tapestry	[ ]	[ ]
Spinning, weaving	[ ]	[ ]
Flower arranging	[ ]	[ ]
Decorating a room	[ ]	[ ]
Rearranging your room	[ ]	[ ]
Restoring furniture	[ ]	[ ]
Making repairs	[ ]	[ ]
Woodwork	[ ]	[ ]
Making a model aeroplane or boat	[ ]	[ ]
Recreational Activities		
Going for a walk	[ ]	[ ]
Lazing in the sun	[ ]	[ ]
Sitting on the beach	[ ]	[ ]
Taking the dog for a walk	[ ]	[ ]
Having a spa or sauna	[ ]	[ ]
Meditation, yoga or tai-chi	[ ]	[ ]
Listening to music	[ ]	[ ]
Reading a magazine, book or newspaper	[ ]	[ ]

	Next few days	Next few months
Going to hear a band	[ ]	[ ]
Going to the movies, theatre, opera or ballet	[ ]	[ ]
Watching a sports event	[ ]	[ ]
Jogging	[ ]	[ ]
Aerobics or gym work	[ ]	[ ]
Gardening	[ ]	[ ]
Caring for indoor plants	[ ]	[ ]
Chess, draughts, dominoes	[ ]	[ ]
Gathering shells, dried flowers	[ ]	[ ]
Collecting stamps, coins or wine	[ ]	[ ]
Having a game of golf	[ ]	[ ]
Playing tennis	[ ]	[ ]
Table tennis	[ ]	[ ]
Squash	[ ]	[ ]
Lawn bowls	[ ]	[ ]
Ten pin bowling	[ ]	[ ]
Cricket	[ ]	[ ]
Indoor cricket	[ ]	[ ]
Horse riding	[ ]	[ ]
Volley ball	[ ]	[ ]
Swimming	[ ]	[ ]
Surfing	[ ]	[ ]
Windsurfing	[ ]	[ ]
Sailing	[ ]	[ ]
Water ski-ing	[ ]	[ ]
Snow ski-ing	[ ]	[ ]
Scuba diving	[ ]	[ ]
Fishing	[ ]	[ ]
Trail bike riding	[ ]	[ ]
Archery	[ ]	[ ]
Exploring	[ ]	[ ]
Bushwalking	[ ]	[ ]
Camping	[ ]	[ ]
Abseiling, rock climbing	[ ]	[ ]
Caving	[ ]	[ ]
Educational Activities		
Going to the library	[ ]	[ ]
Reading a book, play or poetry	[ ]	[ ]
Doing a course	[ ]	[ ]
Learning a foreign language	[ ]	[ ]
Going to the museum	[ ]	[ ]
Going to the zoo	[ ]	[ ]
Doing a crossword or puzzle	[ ]	[ ]
Nurturing Activities		
Wearing something that feels good	[ ]	[ ]
Buying something for yourself	[ ]	[ ]
Buying something for someone you care about	[ ]	[ ]

	Next few days	Next few months
Relaxing in a warm bath	[ ]	[ ]
Facial/nail treatment	[ ]	[ ]
Massage	[ ]	[ ]
Going to the hairdressers	[ ]	[ ]
Buying food you like	[ ]	[ ]
Walking barefoot on the beach	[ ]	[ ]

What If It Does Not Work

If you find that you are not getting any sense of pleasure or achievement from your activities, then you should work out why. Maybe you have started with an activity that is too complex, or you have unrealistic expectations about your performance. Are the goals you are setting yourself reasonable? Are you expecting too much too soon?

Remember that you are learning new skills which take time and effort to master. If you feel down, then you must not expect instantly to do as much as you did when you felt good. Nor will you enjoy your favourite activities as much as you used to.

It may not be possible to complete some tasks due to circumstances beyond your control, such as interruptions. Your focus should simply be on trying to do your best to carry out your plan. Also check out your thoughts. Are you putting down your achievements: 'That's all I did today!', or 'It was nothing special'? More useful thoughts would be 'Each little bit counts', or 'The smaller the steps that I take, the easier it will become'.

Taking Small Steps

To regain your feelings of pleasure and achievement, it is useful to break activities into parts or small steps. Start with the easily achievable steps and work up to more demanding ones. If your aim is to study, then the first task may be reading one page of a book, then one chapter. Getting your pen and paper out and jotting down some ideas may be the next step. Success on the small steps prompts you to take on more of the task.

Prepare a written step by step plan of the task. Separating planning from performing reduces the number of tasks confronting you at any one time.

Ruth had lost her confidence to drive her car. Here is her graded programme which helped her to slowly develop enough confidence to drive again:

Graded Activities

1 sitting in the car
2 starting the car
3 backing the car down the drive-way
4 driving around the block accompanied by a friend
5 driving around the block alone
6 driving to the local shops accompanied
7 driving to the local shops alone
8 driving to a new area at an off-peak time accompanied
9 driving to the same area at a quiet time alone
10 driving to this area at peak hour
11 driving into the city accompanied
12 driving into the city alone

Ruth repeated each step until she felt sufficiently confident to move on to the next. She was delighted at how each of her successes motivated her to move on. She no longer has a fear of driving.

Setting Weekly Goals

When you look at your goals, such as getting back to work, they may seem a long way off. You are like a mountaineer seeing his destination as a hazy peak in the distance. To help reach the peak, the mountaineer sets intermediate targets and each step edges him closer.

When you feel depressed, it is also useful to set intermediate goals as well as final targets. Setting goals on a weekly basis helps you to keep on track, and also gives you the opportunity to reflect regularly on how you are progressing toward your end goal. The chart on p. 62 shows how Peter put goal-setting to good use:

Peter had a job interview lined up for three weeks time, but was feeling unmotivated and discouraged. He claimed that the task of getting to the interview was overwhelming and he felt helpless. He was encouraged to set weekly goals to help plan for the interview.

By keeping to these goals, Peter felt more prepared for the interview. He was also increasing his chances of getting the job. Over the three weeks he started to feel more confident.

GOALS	
WEEK 1	• Confirm attendance at interview • Check interview clothes • Buy a new shirt
WEEK 2	• Visit the workplace • Talk to other people who work in a similar area • Do some background reading
WEEK 3	• Jot down a list of possible interview questions • Discuss these with a friend or the family • Rehearse the interview with someone • Have a dress rehearsal the night before.

Rewards

It is useful to programme into your activity plan various rewards. Having something to look forward to makes completing the activity much more worthwhile. Rewards are motivators, and may include pleasant activities such as soaking in the bath, going to the beach, or materialistic things such as new clothes.

Write a list of rewards, taking cost and availability into consideration. Reward yourself as soon as you can after you have accomplished your goal. For instance, after doing the vacuuming you may treat yourself to a cup of coffee or a walk in the garden. Peter treated himself to a swim after rehearsing possible interview questions. A night out at the movies was his reward for getting the job interview.

Setting Goals and Priorities

Throughout life your goals need to be reassessed. What is an appropriate and useful goal at one stage in your life, such as pursuing a career, may not be relevant during retirement. Letting go of previous goals can be difficult and sometimes distressing. This is why it is a good idea to develop alternatives which are appropriate to your current needs. When people get depressed at various stages of their life, this is often because they have not reassessed and reviewed their goals. This is especially so when the depression occurs in mid-life. At this time many people evaluate what they have and have not achieved. Some people feel that their time is running out and that their own goals have lost meaning. A lack of goals inevitably leads to depression.

Goals should be interesting and challengi... but not overwhelming. They may include spending more time with your children, learning to relax, learning to play golf, losing weight, getting a job, getting fit and so on. Achieving such goals also helps to give your self-confidence a boost.

The table below will help you to balance your lifestyle and to set goals across all aspects your life. Make sure the goals that you set are interesting, relevant and appropriate for you. Think about some short-term, intermediate and long-term goals.

The best way to make these changes is to set priorities. Decide on one goal that you would like to work on first. It is useful to tackle the easiest initially and then move on to a more difficult one.

EXERCISE 7

GOAL SETTING

	SHORT-TERM GOALS Next week	INTERMEDIATE GOALS Next month	LONG-TERM GOALS Next year
Work			
Recreation			
Family			
Friends			
Learning			
Health			

What is your reward for finishing this chapter?

Chapter 5

COMMON FAULTY THINKING HABITS

'There is nothing good or bad, but thinking makes it so'.
SHAKESPEARE

In a previous chapter we have shown the direct relationship between thoughts and feelings: how you think determines how you feel. When you feel anxious or depressed, your thoughts are most likely to be illogical, and everything will seem to be worse than it really is. This is how illogical thinking distorts reality. These distortions cause over-reactions to everyday situations as well as to major events. Many people think in distorted ways some of the time. By carefully examining and changing your thoughts at these times, you can make yourself feel much better, even without changing what has happened.

As well as determining how you feel, your thinking has a crucial role in determining how you react to major events, such as divorce, death or job loss, or to everyday stresses such as being caught in a traffic jam or missing a deadline. By changing your thoughts, you can also modify unhelpful reactions.

This chapter shows you how to identify and correct thinking habits that distort reality. Ten common types of thinking distortions that make coping with problems more difficult are listed below. See if any of these habits are familiar to you. Memorise this list and refer to it whenever you feel upset, tense or down, to see where your faulty thinking lies. The habits described are extreme. Perhaps your thinking styles are less extreme, but they may still contain the same faults.

Thinking Habits that Distort Reality

1 Black and White Thinking– All or Nothing

This style of thinking views experiences as one extreme or the other, with no middle ground. You evaluate events as successes or failures. There are no shades of grey. You see things as absolutes. The black and white thinker is very definite, he will say, 'this will happen' or 'that won't work', leaving no room for possibilities. Words like 'hopeless', 'failure' and 'loser' are common.

Black and white thinking makes you judge your world and the people in it in a black and white way. People are either 'terrific' or 'terrible'. You make value judgements about how good or bad things are, including yourself. You forget that your *judgements are opinions and not facts.*

Life is rarely totally hopeless or completely magnificent. Most of the time, our experiences are variations between these extremes. Similarly, people are never totally one way or another. For example, no one is completely brilliant or completely stupid, totally good or totally evil.

David would often say about his staff: 'they're either for me or against me'. This was a misconception, as there were times when people agreed with him and other times when the same people disagreed. David had a habit of labelling people 'his type' or 'not his type'. His perceptions and judgements of people were very two-dimensional and over-simplistic.

When Katherine's first marriage broke up, she remembers saying to herself:

'I'll never find anyone else. No one will ever really love me. I will be lonely and unhappy for the rest of my life'.

Because her thinking was full of absolutes, Katherine took a long time to get over her divorce. She made many value judgements such as thinking of herself as a failure for not making her marriage last. Her black and white thinking told her that she would never have another relationship because she was so hopeless. Because she believed that she was a failure as a person, Katherine's confidence was undermined in all areas of her life and her work performance suffered as a result. She secretly believed that everyone else judged her the same way, which was of course quite untrue. Many years later, looking back on her first marriage, Katherine saw that she and her husband were poorly matched and it was not surprising that they had problems.

All or nothing thinking can also be seen when Peter tells himself: 'I'm a failure if I can't get a job. Losing my job means I'm worthless.' Peter also thinks that there is no point in trying to help himself feel better as he will always feel like this. He constantly reminds himself that he will never get anywhere and his life is meaningless.

You can imagine the powerful effect thoughts like these have in destroying self-confidence and the motivation to try to improve things.

While your negative thinking may not be as severe, beware of telling yourself that something won't work or that you can't do it.

Reversing the habit

To change black and white thinking you need to develop the ability to be openminded. This is done by allowing for possibilities rather than by making definite statements. Try saying 'may' instead of 'will'; for instance, 'I may have trouble' rather than 'it will be too difficult'.

It is also necessary to remove all value judgements contained in words like failure, useless, hopeless, incompetent, selfish, neurotic and so on. You could replace them with statements like 'I did not do (such and such) as well as I would have liked'.

2 Setting Unrealistic Expectations— Living by Fixed Rules

People prone to depression have very inflexible rules or goals. For example, if a student with a goal of A were to achieve only a C, she might avoid feeling down by lowering this aim and feeling satisfied that she had passed. It seems that people who do not become depressed are better able to cope with problems and disappointment by being more flexible in changing their expectations.

People who become depressed tend to set higher and more unattainable goals than non-depressed people. This ensures that they are doomed to fail in their own eyes. When you think in this way, you will often say things beginning with:

I must . . . (do it perfectly)
I have to . . . (have a completely tidy house)
I've got to . . . (stick at it)
I should . . . (be doing something better with my life)
I need . . . (someone to care for me)

Some of these statements may look reasonable as you read them through now, but when put into context, they become clearly unreasonable.

'Should' or 'must' statements have little practical purpose. They usually remind you of what you're *not* doing and create unnecessary guilt and disappointment. How many times have you heard people say things like, 'I should stop smoking' or 'I should be more organised', when they have little intention of doing anything about it!

Unrealistic expectations occur when you attempt to be perfect and faultless at everything you undertake and in control of all situations. Because you do not allow yourself to feel nervous, insecure, jealous, be late or forgetful, you put yourself down if these things happen. This thinking style results in you having very little patience and tolerance with your own or other's weaknesses and bad habits. If you make a mistake or hurt someone, you will probably continue to criticise yourself long after everyone else has forgotten all about it.

Katherine, a mother of two children under ten years, believed that she must have a completely tidy house all the time. When people dropped by, she felt very embarrassed if there was any mess. She was unable to relax or enjoy her visitors' company because she worried over what they would think of her messy house. Because of this rule, Katherine rarely invited people over during the day and often felt lonely and bored. She tried to impose her unrealistic expectations on her family and nagged her children to tidy their rooms. She was often upset by their lack of co-operation.

Katherine's rule prevented her from enjoying her daily life and caused her unnecessary embarrassment, loneliness and stress. When she set more realistic standards and tolerated some untidiness in the home, she became a more relaxed and happier person with her family and her visitors.

Some people try to impose their unrealistic expectations on others and feel unnecessarily disappointed or let down when people do not live up to their demands. For instance:

You should . . . (understand how I feel).
You must not . . . (be late).

There is no law stating that people should behave in certain ways, just because you want them to. Remember, other people may not have the same rules as you. What you really mean is that you would prefer that people behaved in ways that suited you.

Reversing the habit

These thinking errors can be removed by using phrases such as 'I would prefer' instead of 'I must' or 'I would like to' instead of 'I have to'. When you think in terms of preferences instead of vital needs or demands, you immediately remove a lot of pressure. Compare—

'I would *prefer* to get there on time', with 'I *must* be there on time'.

'I would *like* to try to relax', with 'I *have* to relax'!

'I *should* lose weight and do more exercise', with 'I *choose* to lose weight and begin exercising'.

Decide whether you really want to do it or not. If you have no intention of losing weight, for instance, do not make yourself feel worse by saying that you 'should' be doing so. Accept that you are not perfect (no one is) and you do not have to live up to all your ideals (or someone else's).

If you see yourself as a perfectionist and know that you have difficulty delegating work, it may be useful for you to try to think in terms of what is reasonable rather than what is ideal. Sometimes the extra effort to make an 80% job into a 100% job is simply not worth the emotional strain.

3 Selective Thinking— Looking on the Dark Side

Looking at the world through dark-coloured glasses causes you to remember and dwell on that one unpleasant event, dismissing all the nice things that may have come your way. Eventually, this type of thinking results in the belief that only bad things happen to you. It also puts a gulf between you and others. You wonder why your life is more miserable than other people's lives. You may think of yourself as unlucky or jinxed and believe that most other people are more fortunate than you are.

For example, Peter has been retrenched from only one job, but he keeps dwelling on this dismissal. He has forgotten about his good job experiences. He feels that he is badly done by and is much worse off than others. What Peter doesn't realise is that many people at some time in their lives are retrenched from a job.

People who become depressed tend to compare themselves only with others who are more successful than they are. This means that they always come off second best. Non-depressed people, on the other hand, tend to compare themselves with those who are worse off! This selective way of comparing has the effect of giving depressed people very negatively biased views about themselves.

Here is another example of selective thinking:

For many months after her second marriage, Katherine avoided contact with her mother-in-law. Katherine was upset and angry about a remark which her mother-in-law had made about her. Katherine dwelled on this remark and convinced herself that her mother-in-law did not accept her. She totally overlooked the fact that her husband's mother had been friendly from their first meeting.

Her selective memory recalled only the negative comments and dismissed all the supportive things which had been said.

Peter and Katherine were initially unaware of their filtering habits and believed that their impressions were correct. Later, they were able to challenge these beliefs.

Reversing the habit

Probably the best way to reverse selective thinking errors is to think of something pleasant that happened to you as soon as you notice yourself dwelling on unpleasant things. Writing lists of positive things that have happened in your life, or on a day-to-day basis, can also help.

Remember you are not trying to kid yourself that everything is rosy, but you are developing a more balanced perspective on people and events.

4 Converting Positives into Negatives—Being a Cynic

When you turn a positive experience into an unpleasant or neutral one by not giving yourself credit for your talents or achievements, you prevent yourself from building self-esteem. This style of thinking is very pessimistic and results in you becoming suspicious and cynical of people's motives. A common example is refusing to accept a compliment, by thinking 'what is he after?' Alternatively, you might think 'they are just saying it because they know how bad I feel, but don't really mean it'. In doing this, you are dismissing the compliment and depriving yourself of a boost to your confidence.

Michelle believed that if anyone got to know her they would think that she was a boring person. When people showed signs of caring and took an interest in her, she believed that this was because they were reacting to the front she put on and they would reject her if they got closer.

David was given a bonus for added business he had brought into the firm. He reacted by thinking, 'It was just good luck, I probably won't be able to do as well next year'. These thoughts prevented him from feeling any pride in his achievements.

Reversing the habit

Be aware of instances when you dismiss praise or compliments. Allow yourself to feel pride in your abilities and achievements and realise that you play a part in creating opportunities and pleasant experiences. If something turns out well, give yourself some credit!

You may spend hours imagining the outcomes of your 'what if's' and eventually convince yourself that there are no other alternatives . . . the worst possible is bound to happen and you can do nothing to prevent it! You are constantly alert for the very first signs that disaster is on its way, which makes you overreact to illness symptoms or problems with your family's health.

One of Michelle's aunts became mentally ill in her 40's and she eventually died in a psychiatric hospital. When Michelle suffered bouts of depression, she always imagined herself suffering the same fate as her aunt. This fear made her significantly overreact whenever she felt herself becoming depressed. She would say, 'It's really going to happen this time. This time I won't recover'. Michelle always did recover, although her fears at times caused her a great deal of distress.

Reversing the habit

Correcting this tendency requires that you become a statistician. Now that is not as hard as it sounds! We simply mean that you need to keep sight of the difference between *possible* (0.001% chance) and *probable* (50% or more chance it will occur.) It is possible that you may be struck by lightning, but certainly not probable, so why spend your whole day worrying about it? This is, however, exactly what people do when they catastrophise. Be realistic about your chances before you jump in and assume the worst.

Michelle learnt to reassure herself by thinking:

> Just because that happened to my aunt does not mean it will happen to me. I am in a better position to deal with the causes of my depression and there is more effective treatment available to me.

Other reassuring thoughts might be, 'there is no reason to expect the worst, I will wait until real problems arise before I let myself worry about them'; 'I will think of less drastic explanations for why this has happened'.

8 Personalising—It's All My Fault

This means that you take responsibility and blame for anything unpleasant. If someone you care for is in a bad mood, you will think it is your fault. If a guest doesn't enjoy herself at your party, you will feel responsible and see yourself as an inadequate hostess. If you inadvertently hurt someone you care for, you feel overwhelmed by guilt. You take too much responsibility for other people's feelings and actions, forgetting that they are ultimately in control of their own lives.

Katherine blamed herself for her daughter's poor report card. When the teacher indicated that she was disappointed in her daughter's results, Katherine took this personally, thinking that the teacher was implying that it was her fault that her daughter didn't do well. She convinced herself that she was a bad mother because she didn't take more time over her daughter's schoolwork. When we questioned her more closely, we found out that this in fact was quite unreasonable, as she did give her children a good deal of help. When Katherine's daughter took up subjects which she was more interested in, her performance improved significantly.

Reversing the habit

You must stop blaming yourself for everything that goes wrong and for everyone else's bad moods. You are not really the centre of the universe, and people and events are not influenced by you as much as you think. Nor do people think about you or judge you as much as you assume. Most of the time other people probably don't even notice the silly things that you do or the mistakes that you make.

The best way to avoid personalising is to stop assuming that people behave in certain ways just because of you, and instead think of other reasons why they may have acted that way. If you are unsure or concerned about their behaviour, ask them what is wrong, to check out whether your assumptions are correct.

Once, when visiting her doctor, Ruth noticed that he was not as friendly as usual. She took his behaviour to mean that he was fed up with her and that she was taking up too much of his time. After the visit, Ruth learnt from the receptionist that her doctor's house had been burgled that morning. Subsequently, whenever her doctor seemed preoccupied, Ruth corrected her tendency to take it personally by reminding herself that he also had his own problems.

9 Mistaking Feelings for Facts— I Feel Therefore I Am

This thinking style confuses feelings with reality. You may believe that because you feel hopeless, you are hopeless. Because you feel dull, you are dull. If you feel hurt, you believe that you have been wronged. Realise that feelings, irrespective of how real they are to you, are not objective facts.

When depressed, Michelle is never happy with her appearance and feels unattractive whenever she goes out. She often thinks: 'I'm so plain, how could anyone be interested in me?' Because she believes her feelings, she doesn't believe others when they compliment her and turns away opportunities to feel good about herself. Because she thinks that she is right and others are wrong, her confidence remains low.

Reversing the habit

- Gather evidence to prove or dispute your negative feelings. Train yourself to be objective and rely on facts rather than on feelings. Remind yourself that feeling so does not make it so.
- Keep a daily diary of your thoughts and feelings and record the strength of feelings at the time of the event. Later, you will notice that your feelings usually diminish over time. Facts do not change, but feelings do, so they are not a reliable basis on which to form judgements.

10 Jumping to Negative Conclusions

This distortion occurs when you draw a negative conclusion from a situation when there is no evidence to support it. There may even be conflicting evidence which you ignore. The problem is that you end up with a negative, self-critical interpretation which upsets you.

Common instances include making assumptions about why someone has behaved in a certain way without first checking it out. You assume that other people are looking down on you or rejecting you. This is also called mind reading. You automatically expect the worst to happen without good reason.

Here are some examples:

> This is the second time my friend has interrupted me. They are obviously bored with my conversation. I must be a really dull person to talk to.
>
> My doctor has just passed me in the waiting room without saying hello. She is ignoring me deliberately because she thinks that I'm a hopeless case.
>
> My husband has been spending a lot of time at work recently. He must be wanting to leave me, but he doesn't know how to let me know.

David was asked by his wife's parents to act as mediator in a dispute they were having with neighbours concerning a boundary fence. His thoughts were: 'I will have to deal with difficult neighbours. It will be impossible to make my inlaws see the alternative view. This is going to wind up in litigation'.

In fact, David, as mediator, was able to arrange a compromise and so none of his negative assumptions came to anything.

Some people even launch a counter-attack on the other person, on the basis of mind reading. This can be rather embarrassing if your assumption was incorrect (and it often is).

The danger of anticipating the worst, is that you are more likely to withdraw unnecessarily from situations. Katherine was invited to a dinner party with a group of friends. She worried all week about the dinner and thought:

> I know that I won't enjoy myself. If I try to talk to anyone my mind will go blank and I won't have anything to say. I'm going to look so stupid.

Not surprisingly, Katherine talked herself out of going as she was convinced that her assumptions were correct. She denied herself the opportunity of seeing if she could get some enjoyment from the party. On another occasion, she did go and enjoyed the conversation. She was surprised at how incorrect her predictions had been.

Reversing the habit

Correcting this tendency involves gathering objective evidence. One or two pieces of evidence is not a sufficiently sound basis on which to form an overall firm conclusion. It is necessary to consider alternative reasons that may be causing someone to act in a certain way. It may help to discuss your concerns with someone who is impartial. Remember that you do not know all the facts and it is a good idea to give yourself and others the benefit of the doubt. It is not logical to always end up with a negative conclusion.

Try doing the activity and finding out how it goes rather than stopping yourself with negative predictions. You may be pleasantly surprised. Taking a chance gives you an opportunity to learn and improve. Self-confidence is built up by doing things rather than avoiding them.

Do not automatically assume the worst when there is a range of possible causes and outcomes. Develop the habit of assuming positive outcomes.

EXERCISE 8

Thinking Distortions Quiz

There are thinking distortions in each of the following situations.

(i) Underline the key words which point to the thinking error.

(ii) Record which thinking distortion is operating. Some situations out in columns as shown in the example opposite.

1 Peter is at a busy restaurant with a friend and the waitress is giving them bad service. He thinks 'I must have offended her somehow'.

DISTORTIONS ____

2 Katherine is cooking dinner and burns the apple pie. She thinks 'The whole meal is a disaster'.

DISTORTIONS ____

3 When David arrives at work one morning one of his closest colleagues walks passed and simply grunts. David thinks 'No one is saying hello to me anymore'.

DISTORTIONS ____

4 Ruth is talking with some of her daughter's friends. She thinks 'This is the second time they have interrupted me. They are obviously bored with my conversation. I must be a really dull person to talk to'.

DISTORTIONS ____

5 The manager returns a report which David has prepared. He commented that it was a good piece of work, but there were a few typing mistakes which would need to be corrected before it is ready for filing. David thinks 'He must think I'm stupid for not picking up these errors'.

DISTORTIONS ____

6 Peter is about to go for a job interview. He thinks 'This is my last hope. If I don't get this job it shows what a failure I am'.

DISTORTIONS ____

7 Katherine watches her two children go off to school. She thinks 'I should be happy all the time. I have no right to ever feel down'.

DISTORTIONS ____

8 Ruth has been invited to join her family on an overseas trip. She thinks 'What if the plane crashes'.

DISTORTIONS ____

9 Michelle is about to go to a party but gets cold feet. She thinks 'I feel so dull. I won't know what to say to anyone'.

DISTORTIONS ____

10 Katherine was about to introduce an acquaintance to a group of people but forgets her name. She thinks 'How absolutely embarrassing. I'll never be able to face that person again. She'll never forgive me. I wish I could just disappear. I'll never get over this'.

DISTORTIONS ____

11 Ruth's friends declare their admiration for the ungrudging efforts she put into caring for her dying husband. She replied 'Anyone could have done it'.

DISTORTIONS ____

12 Michelle believes that she can only have a relationship with a man whom she thinks her father would accept. She thinks 'I must get my father's approval'.

DISTORTIONS ____

Answers to the quiz

1 Personalising
2 Overgeneralising. Magnifying.
3 Overgeneralising.
4 Personalising. Jumping to conclusions.
5 *Polaroid* thinking.
6 Black and white thinking.
7 Unrealistic expectations.
8 Catastrophising.
9 Mistaking fact for feeling.
10 Magnifying. Black and white thinking.
11 Converting positives into negatives.
12 Living by fixed rules.

Chapter 6

CHANGING FAULTY THINKING—THE SECRET OF BEING A HAPPIER PERSON

'If thou art pained by any external thing, it is not this thing that disturbs thee but thine own judgement about it . . . And it is in thy power to wipe out this judgement now.'

MARCUS AURELIUS

The previous chapter outlined faulty thinking habits which, when extreme, distort reality. This chapter will show you how to correct distorted thinking so you can feel better.

Most people have negative thoughts from time to time. It is only when they become habitual and extreme enough to create disturbingly unpleasant emotions that it is necessary to analyse and challenge these thoughts.

The good news is that you can learn to use any strong unpleasant feeling as a signal to make changes for the better. Here is the Five Step way to becoming a happier person.

Step One—Record your experiences

Step Two—Recognise your own faulty thinking

Step Three—Challenge your thoughts

Step Four—Use positive goal-directed thoughts

Step Five—Develop other thought control techniques

The idea of changing your whole thinking style may initially seem overwhelming. In fact some people get more depressed and anxious just by thinking about it! It may take time to challenge and correct your old faulty thinking habits but be patient and you will master this skill. Don't expect to be able to use these techniques instantly, in all situations.

Step One—Record Your Experiences

A good way to start changing faulty thinking habits is to set yourself several opportunities each day to reflect on your feelings and thoughts. At times when you feel upset or angry, try to put yourself in the position of a neutral observer who is examining your thinking style.

The Daily Diary

To examine your thinking, it is useful to keep a daily diary of the times you feel down or when you think that you are not coping. Record your thoughts or images at those times. This self-monitoring will help you recognise any faulty messages you give yourself. Writing down your thoughts enables you to be more objective than if you let the negative thoughts buzz around in your head.

Your daily diary should include the following information, set out in columns as shown in the example opposite.

Situation: In this column you give an objective, factual account of what happened. It should not include interpretations or assumptions. An example might be: 'I momentarily forgot my friend's name, just as I was about to introduce her.'

Automatic Thoughts: This column is to record what you said to yourself when you felt upset, depressed, angry or anxious. It is most important that you distinguish between thoughts and feelings. Thoughts are the interpretations you make about what happens to you. For example, you may say 'I felt like such a fool' after you made a mistake. This is a thought not a feeling. The accompanying feelings to making a mistake may be guilt, embarrassment and some anxiety.

Distortions in thinking: This column enables you to identify exactly which thinking errors you make so you may later correct them. How you recognise distortions is explained in chapter 5.

Feeling: This column describes the emotions you experienced in the situation. Sometimes it is difficult to identify specific feelings. You may know that you feel upset, but be unsure whether this is due to anxiety, hurt or anger. To identify your exact feelings, it is useful to use word associations. For instance,

'I'm feeling awful—fed up—irritable—annoyed.'

Strength of Feelings Then: This column rates how intense your feeling was on a scale from 0-100%. If you felt extremely

SITUATIONS	AUTOMATIC THOUGHTS	DISTORTIONS	FEELINGS	STRENGTH OF FEELINGS THEN	STRENGTH OF BELIEF IN THOUGHT
Attending to children and household chores. Cooking dinner.	Why can't I function normally? Why must I take tablets to be normal? What's wrong with me? Will I ever get well? I hate being like this.	Unrealistic expectations. Selective thinking. Magnifying unpleasantness. Catastrophising.	Anxious Depressed Fearful	90% 90% 60%	90%
	CORRECTED THOUGHTS			**NOW**	**NOW**
	I am functioning reasonably well. The tablets are helping me and I won't need them forever. Nothing serious is 'wrong' with me. It's just my negative thoughts. I can feel better if I work at it. No one feels 100%		Anxious Depressed More confident More in control	10% 5% 70% 60%	80%

embarrassed about a mistake you made, for example, you might rate your feeling as 90% intensity. How you felt at the time is recorded in the sub-column 'then'.

The column for *Corrected Thoughts* is where you substitute more positive helpful thought that will enable you to cope with unpleasant situations by removing the distortion. How you construct your own corrected thoughts is dealt with later in this chapter. The example of Katherine's diary shows that her distressing feelings have lessened in intensity as a result of her new thoughts.

Strength of Feeling Now: This records the change in intensity of your unpleasant feelings after you have substituted positive thoughts.

Step Two—Recognise Your Own Faulty Thinking

Are you a black and white thinker? Perhaps you have a tendency to magnify unpleasant feelings? You can identify your own distortions from your daily diary. To recap on Chapter 5, the most prevalent styles of faulty thinking were described as: (1) Black and White (2) Setting unrealistic expectations (3) Selective thinking (4) Converting positives to negatives (5) Overgeneralising (6) Magnifying unpleasantness (7) Catastrophising (8) Personalising (9) Mistaking feelings for facts and (10) Jumping to conclusions.

Use Chapter 5 to help you identify distortions in your thinking style.

Step Three—Challenge Your Thoughts

Why do you believe your own thoughts? This generally occurs for the following reasons.

Quite simply, the more often you think something, the more likely you are to believe it. Many of your automatic thoughts have been with you for years, and because of their familiarity, you are less likely to question them. Your automatic thoughts are based on belief systems taught to you by your family and are often reinforced by friends and society. These learned beliefs will affect how you cope with everyday stresses and more major crises.

Remember that just because an idea is commonly held, it is not necessarily valid or true. Other people's beliefs are not necessarily right for you.

Recognise that many of your thoughts are not facts. They are merely assumptions which determine how you feel and what you do.

How to Challenge Your Thoughts

To challenge your thinking you need to question the logic of your assumptions and find alternative, positive explanations for things. Distance yourself from your thoughts so that you may be objective and rational and this will lead to an improved ability to cope with problems.

Challenging your thinking means critically scrutinising each automatic thought. You must get out of the habit of automatically believing your negative thoughts. Three techniques are involved:

(i) Gathering evidence to prove your assumptions
(ii) Looking for alternative explanations
(iii) Putting the situation into perspective

(i) Gathering Evidence to Prove Your Assumptions

Evidence relies on facts rather than on opinions. Do you have any objective proof that your assumption is correct?

Ask yourself: 'How do I know that what I am thinking is right?' 'How can I find out if what I believe is true?'

Whenever David discovered errors in his work, he assumed that his performance was not as good as that of his colleagues. To find evidence that this was so, he thought about the comments he had received about his work. Most feedback had been positive and encouraging and his work rarely received criticism. An awareness of these facts helped him dispute his belief that his work was not good enough.

To find out if your thinking is logical, you need to test your conclusions against what happens to you. If you believe that you have offended someone, you can test this by objectively examining that person's behaviour towards you. Does it suggest that your negative assumption is true? If so, changes in the way that person treats you should be apparent. What evidence can you find? How significant is it? If you can't find any evidence to support your negative conclusion, what other explanation could there be?

Beliefs may also be challenged by attempting some task that you expect to be difficult. This allows you to see what will happen, instead of being held back by negative assumptions about what may happen. Katherine discovered that when she finally summoned the courage to ask her mother-in-law not to criticise her in front of the children, she received unexpected co-operation. Katherine had challenged her negative thought that there was no point in talking to her mother-in-law because she thought it wouldn't work.

In order to find out if your assumptions are true you may have to ask others for their opinion. David learnt to ask his boss for feedback whenever he felt negative about his performance, instead of believing his automatic negative thoughts.

It is important to weigh up and review evidence for each specific negative thought. If, for example, you were thinking 'this will be too difficult', you could ask yourself 'How do I know it is too difficult?' 'What exactly do I think will be hard?' 'How can I test out this assumption?' One piece of evidence alone is not enough to support a negative conclusion.

Disputing the idea that I'm hopeless and good for nothing

Thoughts of being hopeless and good for nothing often occur from frustration caused by not doing as well as you would have liked. Disappointment is aggravated by unnecessary anger and unhappiness. Blaming yourself and putting yourself down serve no useful purpose. You do not make mistakes on purpose, no one does!

Disappointments and failures create opportunities to learn and develop new skills. Frustrations provide a chance to try alternative approaches and develop resourcefulness. Without such opportunities we would stagnate.

This is how Katherine challenged her thoughts of being hopeless.

Her daily diary showed her that on the few occasions she had attempted to do something challenging, she gave up after making one mistake. Her negative thought was 'See—I just knew that I'd botch things up. I'm no good for anything.'

She recognised that by expecting herself to do everything perfectly the first time, she was being unrealistic. She was also comparing her abilities while depressed with her achievements in the past, when not depressed, which was unfair.

Katherine made lists each day of all her achievements regardless of how small they seemed. These lists gave objective evidence that she was useful and productive and enabled her to dispute her most distressing thoughts of being hopeless.

(ii) Looking for Alternative Explanations

Consider the advantages of adopting an alternative viewpoint. Would you be able to deal more effectively with the problem if you changed your attitude?

Ask yourself: 'Is there a more positive way I could look at this which will help me to deal with the problem and feel better?'

Disputing the idea that 'It's Not Fair'

The disadvantage in thinking that you are being treated unfairly or that things are hopeless, is that it robs you of the motivation to change things or to try again. Dwelling on the unfair or imperfect aspects of your life leads to anger and depression.

When Peter was dismissed from work, he reacted by thinking, 'that's it, I'll never get another job. No one wants me, I'm finished. There's no point to anything. Life is totally unfair!'

Another disadvantage to self-critical thoughts is that they destroy your self-esteem. Why do this to yourself?

The advantage of thinking in a more positive way is that you are immediately in a better position to deal with whatever problem has occurred. Your reactions, rather than being exaggerated and extreme, become reasonable.

When Peter challenged the validity of his thoughts, he was able to develop the following alternative viewpoint:

> 'I'm not finished. I have my whole future ahead of me.'
> 'There is no evidence that no one else wants me.'
> 'I can start looking for other jobs.'
> 'Unfair things happen to everyone, not just to me.'
> 'I don't have to give up just because of one setback.'

By adopting this view, Peter's reactions were less intense and he felt disappointed instead of devastated.

Disputing the idea that you are a burden

This belief is often held by people who are feeling down, as a result of losing self-confidence in being with people. After her husband died, Ruth withdrew from contact with friends because she thought that her sadness would be a burden to them. She believed that her friends would feel uncomfortable if she cried in front of them. She told herself that her friends had enough problems without worrying about her.

Ruth tested her logic by objectively considering how friends treated her. Was she being treated as though she was a burden? After contacting several friends and thinking carefully about their reactions to her, she saw that overall their behaviour was warm and friendly, although a few had not contacted her very often since her husband's death and seemed a little distant. She found that there was little evidence for her assumption.

To help Ruth find an alternative way of viewing her situation, we asked her how she would react if a friend lost her husband. She told us that she would be willing to spend time with her friend, even if her friend was sad and sometimes cried. She also said that she would be concerned about intruding on her friend's sadness and so would be inclined to let her friend make contact when she felt up to it. By reversing the situation in this way, she was able to dispute her idea that she was a burden and find positive explanations for why a few friends seemed distant.

Are your thoughts helping you to achieve your goals?

Negative thoughts will prevent you from achieving goals by destroying your self-confidence.

Michelle's negative thinking prevented her from developing a relationship. When she learnt to challenge her thoughts—'No one thinks I'm attractive. No one cares for me'—she realised that she was assuming that she knew how men would judge her. She remembered instances when men had found her attractive. It was her own behaviour which prevented her from developing relationships, rather than the fact that men did not care for her. Because of her negative thoughts, she no longer put any effort into her appearance and often behaved in an aloof and sarcastic way towards men, in response to her assumption that they did not like her.

Recognising choices

To achieve your goals, you may need to consider other options or modify goals. If you feel continually thwarted and frustrated by not getting what you want, it may be an indication that your expectations need to change.

To combat feelings of helplessness you must be able to recognise which choices you have. Choices are not just preferences but refer to what is available. You choose your goals and you have the power to change them. You can also choose to change the way you think about things.

Happy or sad, the choice is yours!

(iii) Putting the Situation into Perspective

Putting things into perspective is done by answering each specific distorted negative thought with an alternative positive and realistic thought.

Ask yourself: 'Is the problem as bad or as significant as I am making out?' 'How likely is it that the worst will happen?'

To develop a balanced and realistic viewpoint you need to take into account all the things that happen to you, not just the unpleasant ones. To assess the significance of the problem, be specific and put it into context.

David usually became extremely anxious when late for appointments because of the poor impression he assumed this would give. When he stopped to think about it logically, he realised that few people would use his punctuality as the sole basis for doing business with him. He was disregarding his ability as an investment advisor, which was the relevant factor in the impression he gave to his clients.

As you become more practised in identifying faulty thinking habits, you will be able to do it as they occur. This takes time, and initially it is both easier and necessary to write out your thoughts, as any negative thoughts that remain unchallenged may undermine you.

The Mental Debating Team

Changing your thinking is like having debating teams inside your head. There are two teams. One represents the distorted, negative thoughts that you are familiar with. The other team provides the newer, positive thoughts. Each time you give attention to the negative team, you must give equal time to the positive team.

Succeed or Be Damned!

David felt that he was continually under pressure to perform. He was unable to delegate work as he believed no one would do the work as well as he could. He was also unable to stop work on a task until it was finished. This meant he often stayed late at the office or took work home. He believed that whatever he did should be done as well as possible. David learnt to challenge his thinking in the following way:

Question: If I don't get it done perfectly, what does that mean?
Answer: That I'm incompetent at my job.
Question: What do I think will happen as a result?
Answer: That I'll lose the respect of my colleagues and my boss and I'll probably lose my job.

Question:	What does losing their respect mean to me?
Answer:	That no-one thinks I'm worthwhile and I'll never get another job.
Question:	What does losing my job mean to me?
Answer:	That I'm a total failure.

By using this line of questioning, David understood how he had taken a giant leap from assuming that not doing things perfectly meant incompetence, which meant failure. By magnifying the severity of the problem, he had lost all perspective. It was in fact most unlikely that he would lose his job by easing back on his workload. David noted the following in his diary:

Situation	Automatic Thoughts	Corected Thoughts
Preparing a report	The work is not good enough. I'll never be able to finish it. I can't settle down and set aside time to do it properly.	The work is original and quite acceptable for presentation, even if some fine details lack polish. If I set aside time for quiet periods of continuous work, I will feel better about doing it.

What about 'What If's?'

'What if' statements are usually based on fantasy and an expectation that the worst will happen. There is an enormous difference between planning how to deal with difficulties should they occur and simply dwelling on the worst!

A lot of the anxiety produced by 'what if' statements stem from the underlying assumption that you won't be able to cope or change whatever happens. Remind yourself that there are things you can do to remove or relieve the stress of unpleasant situations that may occur in the future. Dealing with the unexpected provides opportunities for growth and learning. Here is how Ruth disputed her 'What if's':

When her husband died, Ruth decided to sell the family home and buy a smaller place for herself. These were her reactions:

Automatic Thoughts	Challenged Thoughts
What if I find it was a terrible mistake?	I will enjoy having less work to do in a new unit. It will be a challenge for me to start a new life.

Automatic Thoughts	Challenged Thoughts
What if I'm lonely when I get there?	It will take a bit of time to get to know the local people. I can visit my old friends and invite them over.
I'll miss familiar people and places.	By getting involved in local activities, I'll begin to feel like I belong.
How do I know that I can trust my ability to make decisions?	There are good reasons to sell my current house and give myself a new environment. Basically, I know the type of place I want.

Will I End Up Insane?

The fear of insanity is prevalent in people experiencing intense anxiety or depression. It is often the reason why people delay or refuse professional treatment. We can reassure you that psychotic illnesses are quite different to anxiety or depressive conditions. Anxiety and depression will not lead to you losing your mind. Unlike people who experience psychotic illnesses, you have the ability to control and change your thoughts when necessary. The more often you practise the techniques in this book, the better your thought control will be. Katherine's diary entry shows how she disputed her fears:

Negative Thoughts	Distortions	Corrected Thoughts
If my mind is causing these feelings, what does the future hold for me? Will I end up insane?	Catastrophising	Depression is causing these feelings. I am not going insane. My mind is okay. These feelings will eventually pass as I change my thinking.

Being Positive

Many people have difficulty in generating their own positive thoughts if they have been thinking negatively for a long time. Below are listed some common negative thoughts. Each negative thought has a correspondingly more helpful alternative way of viewing the situation.

Common Negative Thoughts	Helpful Thoughts
I can't stand it	I don't like it, but I can put up with it, without making it worse for myself.
I can't cope	It seems unbearable but I am bearing it and I can overcome it.
I'm not good enough	No-one is perfect. There are some things I'm good at so who cares if I'm not good at everything.
What's the point of trying?	If I don't try, I'll never know.
Everyone is happier than I am	I have no proof, even though they seem happier. Everyone has problems.
I can't do it	I will find out how hard it is by trying. The more I do, the easier it will get.
Everyone will think I'm a fool	I don't really know what they will think, Why should I worry what they think. They probably aren't taking as much notice as I think.
What if I lose control?	If I get emotional, it's not the end of the world. Everyone gets upset sometimes.
I feel useless because I have to have someone to do everything for me	I can do some things to help myself and make myself less of a burden.
I can't concentrate	I don't have to concentrate on everything. If I relax my concentration will improve.

Step Four—Use Positive Goal-Directed Thoughts

Sometimes just correcting distorted thinking so that it is more realistic is not enough to make you feel more positive. It may help you to feel less depressed, but in order to feel more confident and happier you will need to believe positive thoughts about yourself, your job, your friends, your life and so on.

The more often you repeat positive helpful thoughts to yourself, the more you will believe them and the more automatic they will become.

You can motivate yourself by thinking of the benefits of doing the particular activity that you are finding difficult. Weigh the advantages and disadvantages of giving in to negative thoughts and assumptions.

Because David had a longstanding habit of procrastination, he decided to apply this motivation technique to his report writing.

He made a list of the benefits of writing his reports without the usual long delays:

- I will feel much better if I make a start.
- The reports don't have to be perfect so I will not agonise over details.
- I will feel less stressed if they're done or at least started.
- I will feel more in control of my workload.
- I will be more efficient.

If you have a similar problem, think about the advantages of completing the task rather than the difficulties involved.

Motivation may be aided by setting small, achievable, short term steps which lead to your final goal.

Building Self Esteem

Self-doubt and self-criticism often prevent you from achieving goals by robbing you of the confidence required to initiate activities or make changes in your life. For this reason you need to dispute these thoughts. Building self-esteem by activating thoughts that give you reassurance and confidence is important. We will return to this in Chapter 8.

Step Five—Develop Other Thought Control Techniques

Be firm with your negative distorted thinking habits. Do not let them get away with making you feel bad. Here are some tips:

Refuse to Tolerate your Negative Thoughts

If you cannot think of anything positive on the spur of the moment just say 'I'm not listening to this rubbish.' Get angry with your negative thoughts, which are, after all, your enemy. Tell them to shut up and go away. You do not need them.

Thought Stopping

Whenever a negative thought intrudes, you can interrupt it by calling out the word 'stop' to yourself. As you say 'stop', imagine a large stop sign with flashing red lights. After you have made this interruption, fill your mind with positive thoughts. You could also imagine something in the future which you are looking forward to, or replay a pleasant scene from your past.

Thought stopping distracts you from your negative thoughts. The more attention you give to negative thoughts, the more believable they will seem, even if they are not based on any evidence. As one negative thought usually leads to another, the best strategy is to nip it in the bud. Distressing feelings should be cut off before they take over.

This technique can be applied to very disruptive, obsessive and phobic thoughts. Many depressed people also find it a useful technique. It works because the people using it have identified their negative thinking and they have at their fingertips something constructive that they can do.

Distraction Technique

Another way of preventing unhelpful thoughts is to keep busy and occupied. Go out and visit a friend, go for a walk or do some work. Read Chapter 4 on getting motivated and arranging activities. Do not let yourself dwell on how bad you feel and do not talk about it with others too much.

If a problem requires action on your part and you feel overwhelmed by negative thoughts, that is not the right time to use the distraction technique. Distraction is not a substitute for thinking through the problem and taking practical steps to reduce it. Rather, it should be used when there is nothing you can do to change an unpleasant situation, or when you have done what you can, but worrying thoughts still preoccupy you.

Distraction techniques are useful to stop the anxiety build-up before stressful situations. Minimise anxiety by focusing your attention away from yourself. Think about what is happening around you. If you find waiting difficult, take along a book or a magazine when you go to an appointment. Here are some other suggestions:

- Observe carefully what is happening around you, take particular note of the architecture of the buildings or examine the variety of plants in the gardens as you walk by.
- Watch other people, observe the funny things that people do.
- Hum or sing to yourself.
- Practise relaxation techniques.

You may have your own favourite ways of keeping occupied when you do not want to be distracted by negative thoughts.

Rehearsing the Situation to be Prepared

If preparing for a stressful event, you need to plan your thinking as well as your behaviour. This means thinking about all possible, and probable, outcomes and devising strategies to deal with each.

Think about how you could cope if you became angry or anxious for example. Plan how you would deal with possible unpleasant feelings or unexpected events. Katherine rehearsed for a difficult discussion with her husband which involved a confrontation:

> 'If he gets angry and shouts at me, I will try to relax and remain calm. I know that he will cool off more quickly if I don't react.'
>
> 'If I get too upset and start to lose control of my emotions, I will simply stop and wait until I feel calmer.'
>
> 'If he gets really angry at what I'm saying, I won't take it as a total rejection of me.'
>
> 'I expect that we will feel uncomfortable but it is important for me to say this to him.'

It is not always possible to feel calm and in control. Allow yourself to experience unpleasant emotions without being overwhelmed by them. Think constructively and tell yourself that you can get through it!

Reviewing Unpleasant Experiences Positively

When something has not gone according to plan, regard this as a learning experience. Analyse what went wrong and how you might prevent it in future.

Try to think about positive aspects of the situation. Praise yourself for whatever attempts you made even if you were not completely satisfied with your behaviour.

Watch out for black and white thinking, such as, 'It was a dismal failure' and magnifying unpleasantness 'I looked a complete fool'.

Do not assume that other people's judgements are as harsh as yours, 'Everyone thinks I'm incompetent'. It is much more helpful to think 'I've done as well as most people.' 'Everyone makes mistakes, it's not the end of the world if I do.' Remind yourself that you do not have to be perfect and that you can improve and change your behaviour if necessary.

Worrying Time

If you have negative, intrusive thoughts that you are unable to switch off, try setting aside a half-hour of 'worrying time' each day to limit the time spent in negative thinking. You may wish to write down your negative thoughts at this time. At other times you must attempt to push negative, intrusive thoughts from your mind by using the techniques described earlier.

Delay Reacting Until Your Thinking is Logical

When you feel overwhelmed by strong emotions, it will be difficult to react rationally. In order to give yourself time to challenge and correct any faulty thinking, postpone decisions or judgements until your feelings have settled.

SUMMARY

Learning to Question Your Thinking

Once you have identified your own tendencies toward faulty thinking styles, you can make your thinking more effective in dealing with problems by asking yourself the following questions:

—How do I know that what I am thinking is true?
—Are my thoughts helping me to achieve my goals?
—Are my thoughts helping me to get on with others whom I care about?
—Is my thinking helping me to feel good about myself and my life?
—Is there another way I could think about this?
—What advantages are there in adopting an alternative viewpoint?

Chapter 7

OVERCOMING LONELINESS, JEALOUSY AND SUICIDAL IMPULSES

Loneliness and jealousy are common problems that can lead to feelings of despair and worthlessness which, in turn, can induce suicidal impulses. Fortunately, suicidal urges do not often translate into action, but they are most disturbing to experience.

Because suicidal thoughts and intentions often accompany depression, many people come to therapy with requests for specific methods to help them cope with these experiences.

This chapter examines various factors which create or intensify these distressing feelings and suggests practical techniques by which you can reduce or control them.

Thinking Your Way Into Loneliness

Loneliness is experienced by many people and is often accompanied by thoughts such as:

'I have no real friends.'
'No one likes/loves me.'
'What good am I to anyone?'
'No one really cares for me.'
'Why does no one understand my feelings?'

Thinking in this exaggerated way increases the intensity of your feelings and robs you of motivation to change things.

> 'It felt like I had nowhere to go, nowhere to turn for help, or support, or even to talk about things. I had difficulty in turning my thoughts away from my problems. Outwardly, few people appeared to be aware of how miserable I felt. This made me even more despondent. 'No-one notices me, no-one cares about me' was what I told myself. I constantly drew comparisons in my mind between myself and other people. It made no difference whether I knew anything about their

own situation or feelings, I was convinced that I was somehow inferior. I passed the days, each seeming more meaningless than those before.'

KATHERINE

Comparing Yourself

People who are feeling lonely very often compare themselves with others who seem to have busier, happier lives and more fulfilling relationships.

Michelle always compared herself with the most popular girls at work and thought 'Why can't I be like them?' When she heard others talk about places they had been to or people they had met, Michelle imagined the fantastic times they must be having and judged her own activities as dull and boring by comparison. Her lively imagination was contributing to most of her feelings of loneliness. She imagined that other people had perfectly happy relationships all the time. She assumed that others were always using their time in a satisfying way. Because she saw other people's lives through her distorted imagination, Michelle often felt inferior. There was no way that her own life could match up to her idealised fantasy of other people's lives.

Stopping the Comparison Trap

To overcome feelings of inferiority and loneliness, you should develop more realistic views about how others spend their time. You must also stop devaluing your own activities and develop opportunities for pleasure and satisfaction in your own life. Here is how Michelle stopped devaluing herself:

Automatic Thoughts	Changed Thoughts
My life is boring.	That's not really true. I usually enjoy my work and I like reading and going out. I could make the effort to go somewhere like an exhibition or a movie if I feel bored.
Everyone else has a better time than I do.	I don't know this for a fact. Just because they seem busier doesn't mean they are more satisfied.

Feeling Down Causes Loneliness

Feeling depressed can in itself be a cause of loneliness. When people feel depressed, they place less emphasis on their health, their grooming and appearance. They lose interest in things and often believe that they have nothing to offer. This can lead to withdrawing from social contact or relationships because of the fear of being hurt or rejected. They assume that others see them as dull and uninteresting also. Unfortunately, withdrawing from social contact gives more opportunity for brooding and self-pity. It never seems to occur to them to give others the opportunity to cheer them up!

Four Steps to Overcoming Loneliness

- Determine why you are feeling lonely.
- Challenge thoughts that lead to loneliness.
- Motivate yourself with positive thoughts.
- Set goals.

Step One—Determine Why You Are Feeling Lonely

Loneliness can be the result of not knowing enough people, having problems in current relationships or holding unrealistic expectations about the importance of relationships. Each cause can be worked on and resolved.

(i) A Lack of Relationships With Others

If you have few or no close relationships, and wish to change this, you need to do two things. Firstly, change your thinking so you will be encouraged to meet more people. Secondly, change your behaviour to give yourself opportunities to do so.

None of Michelle's recent intimate relationships lasted longer than three weeks. Whenever a man attempted to show interest, she would reject the idea that he was interested in her and clam up. If he persisted, she was unable to talk with him in a relaxed way. This pattern led each man to believe that Michelle had no interest in him.

(ii) Dissatisfaction With Existing Relationships

If you feel unfulfilled and dissatisfied with current relationships, examine your thinking to discover why and then change your behaviour to improve things that you are unhappy about. This may mean improving your communication and assertiveness skills.

Katherine often felt lonely after communication with her husband had broken down. When she attempted to improve the situation, Katherine thought that her husband did not try hard enough to bridge the gap. Because of this, she felt that there was no intimacy in their times together.

(iii) Anxiety About Being Single

A widely held belief is that you must have someone with whom to share your life in order to be completely fulfilled. Our society, although supposedly liberated, still encourages this attitude. The consequence of holding to this view too strongly is that you may have difficulty coping with periods in your life when you are alone.

Michelle finds it hard to enjoy herself socially because she believes she should have a partner to be socially complete. She also believes she will never find the right man.

Many single people feel low when most of their friends seem to be a couple. They forget that being alone or single is a phase that everyone goes through one or more times in their life! What usually causes the most distress to single people is the assumption they make, that they will never have a relationship, and will have to face the future alone.

The notion of being alone for some people means the same as being unloved or unwanted. Unfortunately for them, being single is not recognised as being worthwhile. The meaning that the word 'alone' has for you influences how well you cope with your life. For instance, if you fear the idea of being alone, you may rush into relationships prematurely, or remain in an unhappy relationship.

How You Can Feel Good About Being Alone

History and the media show us that many people are successful, single and happy. Having an intimate relationship can be very satisfying, but be careful if you are busy convincing yourself that it is essential to happiness. It is not! If you believe this, you are overemphasising the importance of one aspect of your life. All types of relationships can be stimulating and satisfying, not only long-term ones. Similarly, it is possible to find fulfilment through many goals other than having relationships.

Being alone is far better than living in an unhappy, dependent relationship which destroys self-esteem and causes greater demoralisation.

By de-emphasising the importance of a major intimate relationship, you can become free to explore and develop other ways of finding fulfilment and satisfaction in your life. Being alone is necessary to develop your own skills and interests. Without learning to develop resources to please yourself, you will always be at the mercy of others. You will feel just as trapped by a relationship as you feel lost without one.

Developing self-sufficiency improves your self-esteem, with the result that you feel much more positive about yourself and your life.

EXERCISE 9

- Make a list of activities that you can enjoy doing alone and start doing them.
- Make a list of activities that you would prefer to share with someone and try doing them alone.
- Think about the goals you would like to achieve with your life and start working on the ones you can attain.

Step Two—Challenge Thoughts that Lead to Loneliness

This can be done by finding objective evidence, supplying alternative explanations and testing your assumptions.

Believe it or not, loneliness is something that you bring on yourself by your own thoughts and behaviour. You may not be willing to accept this idea, but if you do, you will be in a more powerful position to overcome these feelings. Here are some of the myths that create loneliness:

'It's Wrong To Show Emotions'

Many people assume that if you show emotion over personal problems, disapproval and possible rejection will follow. Feeling down may cause you to withdraw from your usual routines and social activities. The myth that 'other people don't have these problems' is another barrier to communication and gaining support. One person in five suffers symptoms of depression, so you are not alone!

Katherine stopped working and seeing friends when her depression was severe, because she did not want to cry or break down in front of others. Her inability to accept or show any sign of 'weakness' in herself is a tendency in depressed people. Here are her reactions:

Situation	Emotions	Automatic Thoughts
Crying in front of workmates	Embarrassment 100% Guilt 80% Depression 100%	I've made a fool of myself. What do they think of me? I will lose my job.

When Katherine examined her assumption, she remembered that her friends at work had been supportive. She also realised that she had initiated the withdrawal from friends and work.

After challenging her wrong assumptions in the following way, Katherine felt able to keep in contact with people during times of depression. She was able to reduce her unreasonable fear of showing her feelings in front of others, and felt relief when she did, rather than depression. She also found reassurance in the reactions of her work friends.

Assumption 1:	That others will think I'm a fool.
Challenge:	I have no evidence to support this. In fact I have found them to be caring.
Assumption 2:	I will lose my job.
Challenge:	I am a valuable asset. There is no suggestion from my boss that he is unhappy with me.

Situation	Emotions	Corrected Thoughts
Breaking down in front of workmates	Embarrassment 10% Relief 60% Reassurance 80%	I have a good reason for being so upset. I don't need to feel a fool. I won't be rejected for breaking down.

Expecting 'Understanding'

Sometimes, loneliness and feelings of rejection are caused by assumptions about other people's motives. When people feel let down by others, the common thought is 'they don't care'.

Expecting understanding from your family or friends can cause loneliness. This happens because it is not always possible for others to understand your feelings of depression unless they have had similar experiences themselves. Do not confuse understanding with caring. Others may care very much about you, even if they do not fully understand. Expecting people to show care only in the way you want can lead to misunderstandings and unnecessary hurt. The following entry from Peter's diary illustrates this:

Situation	Emotions	Automatic Thoughts
Being told that my closest friend knows I'm in hospital and hasn't rung me.	Anger 70% Hurt 90% Depression & loneliness 80%	My closest friend couldn't give a damn about me. She knows how depressed I've been and doesn't even care. We've been friends for so long. Thanks a lot for nothing!

To assist Peter in challenging his assumptions, we asked him to supply more evidence showing that his friend did not care. In the process, Peter remembered positive and caring actions his friend had shown him in the past. Peter was encouraged to think of other reasons why his friend had not called. He remembered that he had not contacted his friend to let her know that he was in hospital. It was also possible that Peter's friend assumed he did not want her to visit. To test his assumption, he decided to call his friend, who was delighted to hear from him. She had been reluctant to call the hospital, as she felt it would be an invasion of his privacy.

'No One Cares'

Let others show that they care about you in their own ways! If you expect them to do certain things for you, you must tell them. It is not fair on yourself or others to expect them to read your mind and so to know exactly what you want every minute of the day! Caring for someone does not include the gift of clairvoyancy.

Before you let yourself believe the negative things you say, see if you can find objective proof that your ideas are correct. Your proof should be based on facts and not just feelings. If your loneliness stems from thoughts like 'no one really cares for me', see if you can challenge your ideas. Ask yourself 'How do I know that is true?' See if you can think of instances which prove that your negative thoughts are wrong.

Here is an example of how Michelle learnt to challenge her assumptions:

Michelle:	No one likes or cares for me.
Therapist:	How do you know?
Michelle:	Well no one asks me out anywhere or comes to visit me.
Therapist:	Do you mean no one contacts you at all—ever?
Michelle:	Only my family. Other old friends hardly phone.
Therapist:	Has anyone else besides your family contacted you in the last six months?
Michelle:	Well, yes . . . a few people.
Therapist:	Why did they contact you?
Michelle:	To have a chat and see what I was doing. I felt my life was so dull compared to theirs. I had nothing much to tell them. So now they don't phone.
Therapist:	How many people did you contact in the last six months?
Michelle:	Well, my life is so dull. I don't phone people because I can't stand it when they ask what I have been doing. I feel embarrassed to tell them that I've been down and haven't done much. When I see people I used

	to know, I feel that they must be able to tell that I'm depressed because I act so differently. I don't want everyone to know my problem so I'd rather not see them.
Therapist:	So what you're saying is that you are choosing not to make contact with people. Would you keep phoning someone if they didn't seem interested to talk to you?
Michelle:	No, I guess not.
Therapist:	Is it possible that this is the real reason why some of your old friends aren't phoning you as much?
Michelle:	You mean because I don't seem interested in them—they think I don't care for them?

By challenging her belief that 'no one cares', Michelle saw that this was probably not true. She found that what she really meant was that her friends did not contact her often enough.

Through this exercise, Michelle became aware of how her behaviour influenced that of her friends. Even though her friends did contact her from time to time, she was not encouraging, nor did she make an effort to contact them. She was usually passive and let her friends arrange activities. The belief that her life was dull prevented her from telling her friends about her activities. By understanding how her negative thinking affected her relationships with her friends, Michelle was able to see that she was creating the gulf between herself and them.

To put the 'no one cares' belief into proper perspective, consider the difference between other people caring for you and having them take responsibility for your predicament. How you feel is not the responsibility of others. Expecting others to look after your feelings is unfair if you are not making the effort to help yourself feel better.

Overcoming Barriers to Being With People

The table opposite shows some thoughts that prevent you from mixing comfortably with people and the challenges to those thoughts:

Step Three—Motivate Yourself to Overcome Loneliness

When loneliness is caused by a lack of relationships, you may find it useful to think of the positive reasons for initiating social contact

Thought	Challenge
I'm dull and boring	I'm not dull because I have opinions and things to say.
I have nothing interesting to say.	My friends used to listen to what I said so it couldn't have been that uninteresting.
They will ask about my problems and I won't know how to answer.	If they do ask me how I am, I can answer briefly and change the topic.
They should contact me first.	It doesn't really matter who contacts whom, as long as we stay in touch.
They don't care about me anyhow.	I have no proof that they don't care. In fact they have done many things to show they do care. Not contacting me as often as I want is not proof that they don't care.

and what benefits may be achieved by changing your behaviour.

As Michelle wanted to start a relationship with a man, we asked her to write a list of all the reasons she had for initiating relationships with men. This was done to remove the barriers that her negative thinking caused and this is what she wrote:

I would like to have a relationship.

By practising talking to men it will help me to feel more comfortable when I'm with someone new.

I will probably have to go out with a few different men before I meet one that I get on with.

I can still enjoy going out with someone even if I don't want a steady relationship with that person.

The more men I meet, the better my chances are of finding someone I really like.

Michelle also listed some benefits of changing her behaviour:

My confidence in meeting people will improve.

My conversational skills will improve.

I will go out a lot more than I do at the moment.

Going out to different places will give me more to talk about.

Lists like these will encourage you to change your behaviour so that loneliness can be overcome.

Step Four—Set goals

Perhaps loneliness for you is caused by not being busy or involved in activities that give you a sense of achievement. Katherine found that gardening became an absorbing and pleasurable hobby, which gave her a sense of creativity and satisfaction. See Chapter 4 for more hints on setting goals and keeping busy.

You probably feel that part of your loneliness problem is not having many opportunities to meet people. If this is so, try to get involved in activities where you can meet people with similar interests. Michelle enjoyed playing squash, but had not had a game for some time. She decided to join a local club which also had some social functions.

Taking up hobbies or joining clubs may seem difficult if you are down, but Chapter 4 will guide you into taking small steps which will put you on the road to achieving your goals.

Activities to Help Overcome Loneliness

- Dispute negative thinking.
- Design a plan of things to do that you can tick off and feel a sense of achievement when they're done.
- Contact people you know and like. Arrange to meet them.
- Develop a hobby. Your local newspaper, school, phone book or council can assist with telling you what is available in your area.
- Talk to neighbours and local shopkeepers. They are a good source of local news and support.
- Let friendships develop by spending a bit of time getting to know people you work with. Have lunch together or suggest drinks after work.
- Be prepared to go more than halfway to meet and get to know others.
- Become physically active. Get fit, join a gym or sports club. Exercise keeps you busy, healthy and helps you meet people.
- If you are shy, attend a social skills training, communication or assertion training course conducted by a qualified psychologist.

Overcoming Jealousy

'Jealousy is all the fun you think they had . . .'
ERICA JONG

What is Jealousy?

Essentially there are two types—envious jealousy and possessive jealousy.

Envious jealousy occurs by unfavourable comparisons and is reflected in thoughts like:

> 'I wish I had her figure', 'I wish I had his money', 'I wish I had her job'.

Constant comparison with others can be due to competitiveness. A small amount of competition is a good thing for both our work and personal lives, but too much can harm relationships.

Competitiveness often encourages imitation amongst friends. You may mirror a certain lifestyle that you admire in a friend. Imitation, in small amounts, is considered a form of flattery.

Imitation and jealousy become problems when you begin to lose your own individuality through trying so hard to be like others whom you admire.

Another reason for people comparing themselves to others is a lack of satisfaction with their own lives. By copying the lifestyle of others who seem happy and content, the imitator hopes to feel this way also.

Possessive jealousy is caused by the fear of loss. This type of jealousy causes people to become very possessive—of friends, husbands, wives or boyfriends, for example. Others become very possessive about their jobs and will not share information or give assistance to work friends in case their position or status is threatened.

People with intense jealousy may often have obsessive thoughts that they cannot stop. Such thoughts become fixed on a particular person: a partner or lover. If a partner is home late or a lover does not phone when expected, the jealous person becomes immediately suspicious. The obsessive thought may be; 'he's with someone else'; 'he does not care about me'; 'he does not want me'.

Intense and irrational jealousy places great strain on relationships. One young woman told us she was uncontrollably jealous when her boyfriend saw his friends before coming to visit her. She imagined he had more fun with his friends. She also suspected that his friends might introduce him to other women. Her fears caused many unnecessary arguments. Another woman told us she was unable to go out with her boyfriend because he looked at other women. This woman also became annoyed when her boyfriend looked at attractive women on television.

What Causes Jealousy?

In most cases, inadequacy and insecurity, due to low self-esteem, cause feelings of jealousy. Essentially, if you have this problem, you do not think you are good enough and you place insufficient value on yourself and whatever talents you have. If you believe you are physically unattractive, as many people do, you will feel inadequate physically. David's belief that he was ugly caused him intense jealousy whenever his wife casually looked at or had a conversation with another male.

Intense jealousy generally stems from strong feelings of insecurity. Katherine felt insecure in the early stages of her relationship with her husband. She was unsure how strong his commitment was to her. As a result, when he arranged to see friends without her, she would manipulate the situation so that she was included. The effect was that his friends disliked and avoided her. This in turn caused greater insecurity.

Six Steps to Overcoming Jealousy

Step One—Examine Your Thoughts for Errors in Logic

Jealousy often occurs when people confuse attention with caring and interpret lack of attention as a lack of caring. Katherine believed that she needed her husband's attention as proof that he cared. This belief was clearly illogical as it would be impossible for her husband to give Katherine his undivided attention all day. Yet it is quite possible and most likely, that he cares for her 24 hours a day! People show care in many different ways. To avoid unnecessary hurt, be aware of the meanings you place on certain behaviours and the assumptions you make about the motives of others. Check that the assumptions you make do not contain distortions of facts, which are described in Chapter 5.

Step Two—Challenge Your Thinking

Use the technique of gathering objective proof to support your ideas and consider alternative explanations that are more positive and less destructive. Test your assumptions to find out if they are true.

The following example shows how Katherine developed alternative explanations for her husband's behaviour one evening while they were out with friends:

Automatic thoughts

He never looks at me that way.

I've become unattractive to him.

He is finding her more interesting.

He's probably bored and fed up with me by now.

He doesn't care about my feelings as much as he seems to care about hers!

These thoughts led Katherine to feel jealous and depressed. By analysing her thoughts, Katherine became aware that she always expected herself to be stimulating company for her husband. This unrealistic expectation caused her to feel let down when he temporarily found another woman interesting. Katherine was threatened, as her self-esteem was not very high. The meaning she attached to her husband's behaviour was that he found her unattractive and boring. When Katherine challenged these thoughts, she developed a more positive and realistic explanation for her husband's behaviour, which in turn boosted her self-esteem.

Positive Alternative Thoughts

He is having a fun evening. He does look at me in a special way when he's enjoying himself.

At the moment he is more interested in her, but he did talk to me at other times. It doesn't mean anything.

There is no real proof that he is bored and fed up with me even though we don't always have interesting discussions together. He is usually considerate and pays me a lot of attention.

He already knows my opinions on this topic so that is probably why he is listening to her. He is not really ignoring me. I can let others have a say.

Step Three—Build Your Self-Esteem

The important fact to remember is that intense jealousy arises from poor self-esteem and not from how others treat you. You can stop feeling jealous by building your self-esteem, which is described in Chapter 8. Healthy self-esteem will enhance feelings of security that protect you from the destructiveness of jealous thoughts and actions.

To help build her feelings of self-esteem, Katherine challenged her beliefs that she was uninteresting and unattractive. Reminding herself of her positive qualities enabled her to feel less threatened when her husband paid attention to other women. By building her self-esteem, she felt less need to be like others and consequently felt better about being herself. When she stopped comparing herself with other women she became more relaxed in company and she and her husband could enjoy their social evenings.

Step Four—Stop Unfavourable Comparisons

Depressed people tend to compare themselves only with people they judge as superior in some way. This form of self-evaluation means that individuals generally see themselves in a poor light.

To build and maintain good self-esteem, it seems necessary to have a positive bias when comparing yourself to others. Feelings of jealousy can be reduced if you stop dwelling on what is better about others and think about their negative points as well. This will help you develop a more balanced perspective on people and be less envious as a result.

Be Your Own Person

Setting and achieving your own goals is important in reducing jealousy based on comparison. To protect your individuality, determine which goals are appropriate and achievable for you. Achieving your own goals will prevent you from feeling jealous of other's achievements and you will feel greater satisfaction with your own life.

Step Five—Develop Trust

If your thinking is biased towards recalling unpleasant things other people have done to you and minor criticisms and rejections you have received, the consequence is poor trust of others. This leads to negative assumptions about the motives of others. If someone has forgotten a favour that they promised, you may assume that they do not care enough for your wishes and have not bothered, instead of assuming that they were merely busy. You will take things personally when people do not do as you wish, instead of viewing their behaviour in a neutral way.

To develop trust in others you need to:

- be aware of the assumptions you make about the meaning of their behaviour.
- challenge these assumptions by finding alternative, positive, nonpersonal meanings and motives. Examine your thinking for distortions (see Chapter 5) and correct these if necessary (see Chapter 6).
- don't blame others before making an effort to find out the reasons for their actions. You may need to use the assertive skills outlined in Chapter 9 to discover their motives. Don't assume, ask! As a general rule, give others the benefit of doubt. Not everyone thinks as you do.
- actively remind yourself of the times when the person has shown consideration for your feelings.
- think about whether your expectations of others are reasonable, make sure you let them know what you expect and give them the chance to disagree. Other people have different values and priorities.

Step Six—Set Limits On Your Behaviour and Thoughts

If your jealousy has been difficult to control and results in an angry mood that lasts for hours, try using the technique of 'limit setting'. This is how it can be applied:

Decide in advance how long you will allow yourself to be angry. If your habit has been to rant and rave or sulk for hours, put a time limit on this. Initially, you may decide that you want 20 minutes to get your feelings out of your system. When the time allocated has expired, you should then attempt to control and withhold your feelings. To do this effectively, you could try to distract yourself by thinking about something completely different or use relaxation techniques.

As your ability to control your feelings improves, you can reduce the amount of time needed to express them. Twenty minutes may be reduced to 10 minutes and so on, until you are able to express yourself without losing control.

How Partners Can Help

To assist you in limit setting, tell your partner of your time limit and request that he simply accepts your feelings and does not react or disagree with you at that time. To maximise co-operation, stick to your pre-arranged time limit.

The ability to use humour is a real bonus. If you can make the situation lighthearted by saying something like 'okay, I want 20 minutes to sulk!', it helps to distance you from intense feelings and reduces their significance.

Understanding and Beating Suicidal Impulses

> I'm always misunderstood. I desperately need someone to help me find out who I really am. I am unable to find a reason for living. No one cares. They should know, they're my friends. I'm better off dead. My family doesn't care enough, maybe they will when I'm gone. I'm no use to anyone.
>
> PETER

Suicidal thoughts and obsessions are common to many depressed people. Sometimes thoughts of suicide create enormous fear as you may believe that because you are thinking about it, you will do it. Most depressed people do not attempt suicide even if they have thoughts of doing so. If you have attempted suicide in the past, realise that it is not the only solution to your problems. This section provides suggestions for dealing with suicidal thoughts and urges.

Who is Most at Risk?

Suicidal intentions place people more at risk than suicidal thoughts. Intentions involve specific planning as to how they will take their life and making arrangements for their death, such as a will or writing parting letters.

People most at risk of suicide include those who:

- are men
- are socially isolated

- are separated, widowed or divorced
- are suffering serious emotional or physical illnesses
- have very low self-esteem with a tendency for severe self-criticism and guilt. The perceived need to be punished often contributes to self-destructive urges.
- have a previous pattern of poor coping with stressful life events such as a relationship break up or death of a loved one.
- have attempted suicide in the past
- have difficulty expressing anger and frustration in a positive way.

What To Do if You Feel Suicidal

• Identify the specific problem by asking yourself the following questions:

What is making you think about ending your life? Is it the loss of a relationship? Is it a perceived failure in your career? What triggered your thoughts of suicide?

• Investigate alternative solutions

Take steps to change the situation or resolve the problem. Investigate alternatives to suicide. What appears to be an insoluble problem may be looked at in new, more flexible ways. Being flexible increases the probability of finding a solution to your problems. Ask yourself:

> Is there another way of looking at this?
> What can I do to improve the situation?
> Is there anyone who could help me?

One woman began to experience suicidal thoughts during a depression that began after her mother came to visit. Although it was originally intended to be only a few weeks, her mother's visit stretched into several months. During her stay, the mother was very critical of her daughter and openly disapproved of her lifestyle. Because of her mother's criticism, the daughter began to see herself as a bad influence on her own young children. Five months after her mother arrived, she experienced repeated intrusive thoughts about doing away with herself. She felt very guilty that she was letting her children down and guilty for receiving financial assistance from a male friend, as her mother disapproved of this very strongly. Her thoughts about suicide became more and more frequent and frightening to her. As she became worse, her mother insisted on staying to look after her and the children.

To deal with this situation, the woman was encouraged to shift her attention from her frightening suicidal thoughts to their cause. She was able to see that her thoughts were brought on by her guilt, due to her mother's severe criticism and also by her anger towards her mother's behaviour. She had redirected her anger inwards by wanting to destroy herself.

In order to rid herself of her intrusive thoughts, it was necessary for the woman to change the situation by asking her mother to return to her own city. Without her mother's constant criticism, her anger and guilt were greatly reduced. This in turn eliminated her self-destructive thoughts and she was able to feel much more positive and in control of her life, by standing up to her mother and asserting her own opinions.

• Identify your feelings

Are intense feelings of anger, guilt or depression causing you to think of suicide?

What can you do to change your feelings? Perhaps talking things through with a friend or therapist will help you to find a new perspective. Being able to express your anger verbally rather than in a self-destructive manner will help.

• Identify your thoughts

You may believe that you have let people down or that your actions have seriously harmed those that you care for. Severe self-critical and self-punitive thoughts create intense guilt.

Poor self-esteem makes you vulnerable to suicide attempts as it causes you to be extremely sensitive to criticism, rejection or failure. By building self-esteem you can protect yourself from feelings of worthlessness that can lead to thoughts of suicide.

EXERCISE 10

Think about a time in your life when you were happy or felt worthwhile. Write down what qualities or talents you had then. Now remind yourself that you are still that same person, those qualities and talents are still within you.

Suicidal thoughts are also the result of intense feelings of hopelessness. You may tell yourself that your life has no meaning or purpose. You may believe that there is nothing you can do to make your life happy or worthwhile. It is most important that you recognise that feelings of hopelessness are a symptom of a depressive illness and are not based on reality. These feelings will lift as your depression is overcome. The intensity of your feelings reflects the severity of your depression, not the real condition of your life. By obtaining treatment you can make these feelings diminish and if your treatment to date has not been effective, try another approach. Change doctors, therapists or medication. Effective treatment is available. You need to find what works for you.

EXERCISE 11

Think about all the positive things in your life and the people you care for. Ask them what they like about you and why they want you around.

Write down all the things you have achieved in your life so far.

Think about the effect your suicide would have on people you care for.

• Dispute your negative thoughts and assumptions

Here is an example. Write down your own substitute thoughts and try to develop positive alternatives.

Thoughts	Challenge
I wish I was dead because I can't stand another day.	I don't really want to be dead. By getting help there is a chance that things will improve.
What's the point of living like this?	I have felt happy in the past and that my life was worthwhile. It is possible that I could feel that way in the future.
I want to destroy myself.	I don't really want to destroy myself. I want to feel worthwhile.
If we're all going do die anyway why bother struggling on?	There must be a purpose to our lives. I want to feel content and that I have achieved something by being here.
There is nothing left for me to live for.	I have my children whom I care for very much. I have a responsibility to them as they mature. I look forward to when they will have their own children. I love the sun and nature. I have good friends. I can look forward to feeling better.

• If you have made plans for your suicide, seek help immediately

Talk to someone about your intentions. You need your family and friends at this time. Do not isolate yourself. If you have no one to talk to, phone Lifeline, you local doctor or a community crisis centre. There are other solutions to your problems besides suicide.

Chapter 8

BOOSTING YOUR SELF-ESTEEM

'Seek not abroad, turn back into thyself,
for in the inner man dwells the truth.'

ST. AUGUSTINE

This chapter examines how attitudes towards yourself can affect your moods and offers suggestions for improving self-esteem and self-confidence.

Self-esteem and self-confidence are terms which are often regarded as synonymous. However, Virginia Satir[1], an eminent family therapist, makes an important distinction between the two concepts.

Self-esteem refers to how you judge yourself. It is based on personal values and underlying attitudes which affect how you react in various situations. Examples of positive beliefs that enhance self-esteem are:

It is okay to have limitations in what I can do.
I know I'm a worthwhile person, I don't need to prove that.
I can accept the mistakes that I make and retain my self-respect.

Self-confidence is developed by specific things that you do. You build up confidence when you obtain some sense of satisfaction or achievement by attempting tasks that are challenging. You may not feel confident when you play golf for the first time, but after practice your confidence will probably improve. When depressed, your self-confidence undergoes a set-back, and you feel less able to perform as well as you would like to.

Belief Systems and Self-Esteem

Personal values and beliefs determine the way you interpret situations, which in turn affects your self-esteem. Helpful beliefs allow for flexibility in your experiences and thus enable you to maintain self-respect.

Many people, however, adopt beliefs which have adverse effects on their self-esteem, such as 'To be worthwhile I must do things perfectly'. This inflexible belief might make you feel that you are not doing well enough to earn self-respect. It takes some effort to identify the particular biases in your belief system, but it is worth pursuing, because low self-esteem is the basic cause of most negative emotions. A poor self-image will transform a trivial mistake into feelings of personal inadequacy.

Ruth's belief was that in order to feel worthwhile, she had to be needed. During her husband's illness she felt very needed in her role of caring for him. After his death she felt that she had lost her purpose in life and this caused her depression. In order to feel better, Ruth had to challenge this belief and develop alternative ways of feeling good about herself.

Beliefs that Rob People of Self-Esteem

Here are some of the most usual beliefs held by people who are vulnerable to depression:

- I must prove that I am worthwhile through my achievements.
- I must do things perfectly or not at all.
- I must have everyone's approval all the time.
- I need to be loved by someone in order to be worthwhile.
- The world must be fair and just.

Let's look at these in more detail.

1 Self-Esteem Based Solely on Achievements

Many people attempt to earn self-esteem through their achievements. They may believe that rising to great heights in their chosen career or excelling at a sport gives them the passport to feeling worthwhile. Yet they are quite mistaken. Winning a game of squash, for instance, only means that you played better on that day than your opponent. It doesn't mean that you are a better person.

People who base their self-esteem only on the things they do, put themselves under great pressure as they attempt to get through an endless list of accomplishments. The striving becomes the goal and they are never satisfied. They miss the chance to stop and feel good about what they have already done, as they are too caught up in working towards their goals. They are living in the future, to the exclusion of the present.

When Michelle was asked about her achievements, she wrote out a long list ranging from her university degree to her certificate as a sailing instructor. She had obtained fleeting satisfaction from these achievements but she had immediately set herself other goals. Nothing she did was ever good enough and she was forever trying to improve herself. Her accomplishments were designed to impress others rather than to satisfy her own needs.

To overcome the belief that self-esteem is based only on achievements, it is necessary to find fulfilment in the present as well as from future goals. It is important that you make today as rich and rewarding as you can. You can do this by becoming aware of what you already have and what pleasures are yours on a day-to-day basis. Put more emphasis on the here and now. Arranging your life now so that you are doing what is important for you, will lead to happiness.

2 Striving for Perfection

Your productivity and sense of achievement are enhanced when you aim to do things well. This is very different from *having* to do well. The former brings satisfaction, but the latter leads to temporary relief followed by frustration at having to achieve such high standards again.

People who attempt to do things perfectly are often motivated by the belief that this is what others expect and their efforts are seen as a major way of getting approval. We will examine these ideas more closely to demonstrate why they are unsound.

How to function less than perfectly and be happier

- **Realise when your expectations (or the expectations of others) are unrealistic and remind yourself that you do not have to agree with them.**

A woman who made bridal dresses for exclusive boutiques put herself under considerable pressure to sew them perfectly because they were very expensive. The demand for the dresses increased and so did her workload. The woman worked harder and harder to keep up with the orders, while maintaining her performance at 100%. This proved impossible and she eventually gave up the job, believing that she had failed yet again. With some guidance, she realised the impossibly high standards that she had been trying to live up to and became aware of the unrealistic expectations her employer had of her. She realised that it was her boss's responsibility to make adjustments in the number of staff employed if more good quality dresses were to be produced.

- **Become aware that you do not become more valued by doing things perfectly; you just become more overworked and frustrated**

Michelle tried to impress her boss by being diligent and fastidious in her work. In order to achieve high standards she started work early every morning and stayed back late. A promotion came along and Michelle missed out. Why? Because her boss thought that she was finding the demands of her current job too difficult. Had she tried less hard she may well have got the promotion.

- **Regard mistakes as opportunities to learn**

Mistakes are fundamental to learning better ways of approaching similar situations in the future. By seeing your behaviours as experiments you can gain information and adjust accordingly. This prevents you from judging your actions as either successes or failures.

- **Learn to enjoy your experiences in the present, rather than being preoccupied with the end result**

The notion of flowing with the current and making the most of the present time forms the backbone of many philosophies including Buddhism and Taoism. How often do you catch yourself worrying about the past or contemplating the future and in doing so miss out on the present? This is one of the great shortcomings of being a perfectionist. Focusing on what is happening in the present will help you to tune in to the pleasant and interesting things happening around you.

- **Paradoxically, one significant way of improving your performance involves lowering your standards**

Instead of aiming for 100% all of the time, try aiming for 70% or 50%. If you attempt to do reasonably well and to enjoy yourself at the same time, then you are more likely to relax. If you focus on more than just the standard of your performance, you may also obtain more satisfaction from the activity than you anticipated.

David became irritable with himself when he didn't play well at tennis and was worried about letting his team down. We suggested that he aim to get 70% of his shots in rather than 100%. After some persuasion to experiment with this, David was quite surprised. Not only did he get less worked up and angry with himself, he actually enjoyed the game more. By lowering his expectations he was able to relax, which in turn improved his performance. He learnt to focus on the purpose of the game, which was exercise, and company and fresh air, rather than the standard of the game. After all, mediocre players can enjoy themselves just as much as very good players.

- **Test out for yourself whether you have to do things perfectly in order to achieve satisfaction**

David found that the amount of satisfaction he felt was not necessarily related to how well he performed.

Use the following method to discover that satisfaction and pleasure can be obtained without having to do things perfectly.

Activity	How effective was your performance 0-100%	How satisfying was your performance 0-100%
Induction of new staff	60% (omitted some things I would have liked to have said but ran out of time)	80% (Pleased to meet the new staff)
Sailing lesson	20% (fell overboard!)	90% (Enjoyed the day and overcame my fear of drowning)
Submitted planning report	95% (pleased with the the ideas)	50% (Unhappy that I spent so many evenings working on it)

Burns Anti-Perfectionism Sheet

- **Giving up procrastination:**

People who procrastinate are generally perfectionists. The belief that everything must be done thoroughly or not at all causes decisions and action to be put off. This habit can be broken by planning what you would like to do and how much time should be spent doing it. Try not to take on too much at once. If you set yourself one hour each day to work on something, make sure that you keep to this. Motivate yourself by thinking about the advantages of attempting each task. Chapter 4 guides you further in setting small steps and scheduling activities.

- **Stopping unnecessary checking**

The compulsive need for re-checking is a habit often experienced by perfectionists. Often doubts are held about whether the work done is good enough and whether mistakes have been overlooked. If you have this habit you can break it by:

- keeping to the time allocated for the task
- telling yourself that the work does not have to be perfect
- asking yourself whether it would be considered adequate by most other people's standards
- learning to tolerate the anxiety of not giving in to perfectionist thoughts and behaviours
- distracting yourself by becoming busy with another activity or relaxing until your anxiety levels are reduced.

3 Self-Esteem Based on the Approval of Others

The need for approval starts from the messages received in your early years from your family and other significant people. For example, 'You must do as we wish, in order to gain our approval'.

If you have poor self-esteem then you will probably view yourself through other people's eyes. This leads you to become too dependent on the praise and the comments of others, because you believe that your own judgements do not count. If someone is critical of you or fails to appreciate what you have done, you may think there is something wrong with you, and feel let down. You will also be vulnerable to others by letting their attitudes and moods influence your feelings and behaviours.

How to handle criticism

- **Recognise that your worth is not completely based on what you do**

If someone criticises your behaviour it does not make you a worthless person. Do you know anyone who does everything right all the time? If you think you do, this is probably an illusion! Think about things that you do well and personal qualities you have, such as a sense of humour or generosity, that make you a worthwhile person. What you are is just as important as what you do.

- **Remember that people's judgements about your behaviour are only their opinions which may or may not be valid**

What other people think and say may be unreasonable as a result of their negative thinking.

- **Consider alternative ways of handling criticism**

If you think the criticism is true, consider how you could improve or change in the future. You may wish to ask your critic for more specific advice. Feedback can be used constructively and criticism can be an incentive to change certain behaviours.

- **Decide what is important for you, in your life**

Realise that you can't have everyone's approval all the time as everyone has different values, priorities and opinions. It is necessary to decide what is important for you.

- **Avoid exaggerating or magnifying the incident**

If you have been criticised, it can be useful to distract yourself by involvement in other activities. You will find that when some time goes by the incident will probably not seem so serious.

How to handle rejection

Everyone faces rejection from time to time. Here are some suggestions for dealing with it.

- Remember that, if caused by anger, the rejection may be temporary and when the person cools down you may be able to resolve the problem.
- Recognise that not everyone will like you, nor will you like everyone you meet. This is a reality of life.
- Falling out with a particular person does not mean that you will not have other satisfying relationships in the future.

- Remind yourself that you will eventually get over the anger and disappointment. Don't build it up into a catastrophe as it will only take longer to overcome.
- Remember that the person is not rejecting all of you, rather just *some* of your behaviour.
- Problems in relationships can occur for many reasons. Don't oversimpify the situation by blaming yourself or the other person if your relationship breaks down.
- Consider what you can learn. Are there some characteristics in yourself you would like to change to improve your relationships?
- It is important to be able to reject others, as well as learning to cope with rejection. If you have difficulty saying 'No' it is probably hard for you to accept 'No' from others. Essentially this is just a statement of preference and an opportunity for other people to have their opinions. As you become more comfortable saying 'No' it will become easier to accept this from others. Be careful to avoid reading more into the situation than was intended.

4 Believing that You Must be Loved or Needed in order to be Worthwhile

Some people are convinced that unless they are in a relationship, life is not worth living. To be worthwhile they assume that they need someone else. You may believe that there is no use doing things unless there is someone to share them with. Inevitably such thinking leads to feelings of loneliness, hopelessness and resentment. It also may increase dependency on others and your behaviour may appear desperate or overbearing.

If you believe that you must be loved to be worthwhile, then you have some important work to do. Start by considering the following points:

- **Having a relationship may be something that you want but it is not a need.**

To live we need air, water, food and shelter but we do not need a relationship. You do not need a relationship to be happy, let alone to survive. Many people experience less depression when they leave unsatisfying and unhappy relationships. Relationships are not necessary or sufficient in themselves to gain happiness. If you regard being in a good relationship as a goal or preference, you can take steps to increase the chances of this happening. If you prefer to be alone, allow yourself to feel good about this choice and make the most of it. If you are alone and it is not your choice, make sure that you are not worsening the situation by faulty thinking.

- **There is a major difference between being alone and being lonely.**

Being alone can be a positive and enriching experience. It gives you the opportunity to develop your talents and resources and to learn to enjoy your own company. If you are interested in what you are doing, then you will be more interesting to others. The first step in developing a good relationship with others is to develop a good relationship with yourself.

- **You can enjoy things on your own.**

Another trap you may need to watch for is the tendency to give up certain activities because you are not in a relationship.

EXERCISE 12

Take some time to make a list of pleasant activities which you can do whether or not someone is with you. Experiment to see if you can enjoy yourself while doing some of these things alone. Your list might include going to the movies, museum or zoo, going for a train ride to the country, and so on.

5 Believing that the World should be Fair and Just

If you believe that you are entitled to success, happiness, a relationship and so on, then you are setting yourself up for considerable bitterness and resentment. This is because the world is not always fair. From time to time we all face situations which seem unfair or which do not go as we had hoped. How you cope with things not turning out well is called frustration tolerance.

How to improve your frustration tolerance

If you know that you get easily impatient and frustrated, you might find it useful to work through the following steps:

- **Learn to accept responsibility for your own feelings and actions.** It is not the events around you that make you feel frustrated or angry. Even when something unfair occurs, it is the *meaning* you attach to this that determines your feelings.

Taking responsibility for your frustration and anger has several advantages. It gives you the opportunity to retain control over your feelings and actions. It also allows you to increase the chances of situations working out the way you would like them to. Taking no action while complaining that society is unfair serves no purpose. Taking responsibility means increasing your power and influence over what happens to you.

- **Realise that there will be times when you do not get what you want or deserve in life.** Try to regard unfair incidents as merely disappointing, nothing more. They happen to everyone not just you! If you think 'Why me?', then this will lead to an over-reaction. Frustrating and unpleasant experiences are permanent setbacks only if you choose to see them that way. Ask yourself if the incident will seem as significant after some time has passed.

- **Search for creative solutions.** Rather than dwelling on the incident, it is more productive to search for possible solutions or ways to prevent the incident from occurring again. In this way, feelings of helplessness and frustration are reduced.

- **Ensure that your expectations are realistic.** You become frustrated when you do not get what you want or expect. Therefore, it is necessary to ask yourself whether your expectations are realistic or whether you are aiming for an ideal. Being realistic in the goals you set enables you to deal with unexpected changes.

- **Make sure that your goals are flexible.** You may need to adopt new goals if the old ones cannot be attained. Being flexible extends your options and reduces stress. If plan A doesn't work, then try plan B. This can apply to everyday frustrations or to major crises. If you are running late, an alternative to rushing would be to telephone and give a changed arrival time. If certain plans are prevented or delayed, you can avoid unnecessary disappointment or stress by revising what you wish to do. You will always have other options if you look for them.

- **Remind yourself to be patient and to keep your ultimate goals firmly in mind.** By accepting that delays and setbacks happen to everyone you will be encouraged to keep working on important goals and you will probably be rewarded for your efforts. Try to convince yourself that there is no urgency.

How to Improve Self-Esteem

Improving self-esteem using Cognitive Therapy is quite straightforward. There are just a few simple steps to follow:

Step One—Stop Trying to Prove Yourself

It is one of the basic premises of Cognitive Therapy that all human beings are worthwhile simply because they exist. No-one is any more or less worthwhile than anyone else. Therefore, it becomes pointless to prove that you are worthwhile. While you are preoccupied with attempting to satisfy an unreasonable belief, such as 'I must be perfect', you are missing the more important things in life.

The first step in improving your self-esteem involves accepting and loving yourself for what you are. Be yourself and enjoy your experiences.

Step Two—Challenge Your Negative Thoughts

Only your thoughts about yourself and your experiences can affect your self-esteem. Self-esteem cannot be damaged by the way people treat you, unless you let it. To improve self-esteem you need to detect the distortions in your negative automatic thoughts (which are the everyday examples of your personal values), vigorously challenge them and adopt more realistic thoughts.

To understand which personal values and beliefs are leading to your depression, David Burns[2] has detailed a useful method of enquiry. It involves four stages:

1 Record your negative automatic thoughts.
2 Ask 'If this automatic thought is true, why would it upset me?' or 'What would it mean to me?' Your answers to these questions are other automatic thoughts.
3 Continue to ask the same questions until you have uncovered the beliefs underlying your depression.
4 Challenge the negative automatic thoughts and devise positive rational responses for each.

This process is illustrated in the following example:

While out shopping with her husband, Katherine spent quite a lot of money on a new dress. Her husband remarked 'How extravagant you are!'. Katherine immediately felt guilty, anxious and depressed.

Automatic thoughts	Positive responses
I shouldn't have bought the dress. He probably thinks I'm a fool.	I didn't spend hundreds of dollars, so I'm not extravagant. I know that I can afford the dress. He was probably joking or he could just have cheap tastes!
Q If he did think this, why would it be so upsetting to me?	
A It would mean that he wouldn't want to have anything more to do with me.	Just because I bought an expensive dress, doesn't mean that I'm uninteresting or a fool nor does it detract from the qualities he likes in me.
Q If he rejects me what would that mean to me?	
A It would mean that I'm a failure at relationships.	If our relationship breaks up it doesn't mean that I'm to blame. It takes two for a relationship to work.
Q If I'm a failure at relationships, what would this mean to me?	

Automatic Thoughts	Positive Responses
A It would mean that I'll never have a good relationship and will spend the rest of my life alone.	If this relationship doesn't work out, it doesn't mean that I won't have other good relationships. I could try to learn something from this one and increase my chances of better relationships in the future.
Q If I do spend the rest of my life alone, what does this mean to me?	
A If I can't be loved then it means that I'm worthless.	I don't have to depend on someone or be in a relationship to be a happy and balanced person.

The belief that caused Katherine to over-react to her husband's comment was: 'I need to be loved by someone in order to be worthwhile'.

EXERCISE 13

Choose an example of your own and follow through the four stages to determine which personal values and beliefs may be bringing about your feelings of depression.

Step Three—Be Definite About Your Positive Points

When depressed, modesty is definitely not a virtue. You need to be able to acknowledge your talents and achievements and feel good about them. This is not being egotistical! Positive true statements that you can make about yourself and your life are the building blocks of self-esteem. Each self-defeating thought that you have needs to be followed by a thought that reminds you of your good points and the good things in your life. Make up these statements at a time when you feel good about yourself and read them again when you feel down. Some people keep a copy in their handbag, briefcase or pocket for ready reference.

You could also make a positive thinking tape with your favourite motivating thoughts. The more you practise, the more automatic this way of thinking will become.

EXERCISE 14

When creating positive thoughts, be definite. Rather than saying something vague such as 'I think I have a sense of humour', say 'I know I am witty at times'. Rather than 'I guess I'm as bright as some people', say 'I enjoy my job and I know that I am competent'.

Some positive thoughts

I'll take this one step at a time
I don't have to be perfect
It's okay to be impatient/selfish/lazy at times—that is part of being human
I'm generous with my friends
I'm a good teacher/builder/mother
I'm very caring with my family
I usually finish things which I set out to do
I have achieved some good things in my job and personal life
I will try to keep working on myself
I know that I can look nice when I get dressed up
I know that certain people enjoy my company
I have some good friends.

EXERCISE 15

At the end of each day make a mental note, or write a list of ten positive thoughts about yourself and your experiences. The advantage of doing this is that you are concentrating on what went well, rather than dwelling on the worst parts of the day as there is a tendency to do when you feel depressed or stressed.

Step Four—Respect Yourself

To do this, treat yourself as you would a friend. If you respect yourself, there is a much greater chance that others will too. Allowing yourself pleasurable activites and giving yourself rewards, such as praise, are ways of showing respect for yourself. Don't put yourself down in front of other people.

With a bit of work you can become a happier and more self-respecting person which will help to shield you from depression in the future.

Chapter 9

TAKING CONTROL OF YOUR LIFE

> *If you haven't the strength to impose your own terms upon life, you must accept the terms it offers you.*
>
> *—T.S. Eliot: The Confidential Clerk*

This chapter looks at the difference between being active and passive in managing your life and examines how your behaviour with people affects the way you feel. Poor assertive skills lead to depression and loss of self-esteem. To successfully prevent bouts of depression you need to be assertive. This chapter will show you how.

What is Assertion?

Generally speaking, assertion is the ability to stand up for your rights. We believe that assertion also involves the ability to express your feelings appropriately and without damaging others. The ability to be assertive includes the consideration of the rights and feelings of others as well as your own. Being assertive means that you see yourself as equal to others, not superior (which is aggressive) and not inferior (which is unassertive). Assertive behaviour is usually rational and reasonable.

The ability to stand up for your feelings and rights is essential to gaining control of your emotions and life. Learning to express feelings before they build up in intensity and become overwhelming helps you stay in control and prevents depression. Dealing with problems and grievances as they arise is usually much more effective than postponing action and stewing on things.

Assertive skills to do with communication, problem-solving and dealing with conflict are learnt. They are reflected in both your language and your actions. Many people do not receive adequate training in these skills from their parents or other significant people in their childhood. For example, if you were not encouraged as a child to express your opinion or to disagree with parents, this can lead to difficulties in later life when such skills are required.

I'VE BOUGHT YOU a BOOK ON aSSERTIVENESS TRaINING.
I REALLY DON'T THINK I...
READ IT!
YES, DEaR...

What is Aggression?

When you behave aggressively, you are probably standing up for your rights and feelings, but at the expense of other people. Being aggressive usually means that you are imposing on others, denying them their rights and putting them down in the process. Aggressive behaviour is unreasonable and irrational because it reflects a loss of control.

The Difference Between Anger and Aggression

Many people confuse anger with aggression. Anger is a useful feeling that usually causes you to make required changes. Assertion and aggression refer to the manner in which you deal with your feelings.

Losing Control: The Unassertive/Aggressive Shuffle

If you are irritated by something and choose not to act directly to resolve it, your irritation may grow and you become a time bomb. Eventually the smallest annoyance can set you off. The more feelings you had bottled up, the greater the explosion and loss of control. Guilt, self-criticism and anxiety often follow. You may be concerned that you will lose control in the future and so not speak up when next you feel annoyed. The cycle then repeats itself. Can you recognise this pattern in yourself?

The Problem of being Unassertive

Not expressing feelings directly causes stress and tension. Replaying situations in your mind maintains the built-up anger and makes it difficult for you to relax or concentrate on other things. Sleeping problems can occur as a result.

Your unexpressed feelings may also lead to depression from putting up with things that you feel are wrong. Avoiding your problems can in turn produce feelings of helplessness which are associated with depression.

Aggressive and unassertive behaviour result in loss of self-confidence and depression and both habits can also lead to loss of control. Aggressive behaviour causes loss of self-control and unassertive behaviour causes loss of control of the situation.

Assertive behaviour involves treating yourself well and doing the best you can to ensure that others will also treat you this way. By expressing your feelings and opinions, you have a better chance of resolving conflict, even if you have to compromise to get some of what you want. Assertive behaviour helps you feel more in control of situations and this reduces stress and depression. Research on depression indicates that assertive behaviour can help to prevent further experiences of depression.

Why Assertive Behaviour Varies Across Situations

Assertion is not necessarily a constant behaviour from one situation to another. How well you express your feelings, thoughts and wishes can vary. For example, you may be assertive in your workplace but quite unassertive in personal relationships. How assertive you are varies according to several factors:

(i) Your anxiety level in a particular situation affects how well you are able to express yourself. Your anxiety is produced by your negative thinking in the situation.

(ii) How much practice you have had in being assertive in that particular situation also affects your ability to be assertive. For instance, some people have had limited practice at being assertive with their parents.

(iii) The role models you had, both as a child and adult, influence the way you relate to people. We learn our communication techniques from our parents and teachers.

(iv) Your thinking in a particular situation also greatly affects your ability to be assertive. Perhaps your thinking is hindering rather than helping you to express yourself. For example, if you think you will sound petty, you probably will not speak up. If you call the same point reasonable, you probably will speak up.

EXERCISE 16

How Assertive Are You?

This questionnaire will help you to determine whether you could benefit from being more assertive. Read over the list of behaviours and rate in the column alongside how likely it would be for you to act in this way.

Code	0	Not at all likely
	1	Unlikely
	2	Likely
	3	Highly likely

Behaviour	Likelihood of me doing it
Initiating conversation with a stranger at a social gathering	________
Asking questions of a speaker at a lecture or seminar	________
Complimenting someone you don't know well	________
Asking someone out	________
Being able to refuse an invitation without making an excuse	________
Being able to say no to a favour asked of you by a good friend when you really don't want to do it	________
Being able to dthe isagree with or question criticism you receive at the time it is given	________
Letting a good friend know that their behaviour has upset you	________
• Usually speaking in a soft voice and having difficulty raising it	________
Being able to initiate sexual advances	________
Being able to resist sexual advances comfortably	________
Keeping good eye contact with people you are disagreeing with	________
Being able to disagree without feeling guilty or overly upset	________
Expressing anger without losing emotional control	________
Expressing affection without embarrassment in front of others	________
• Always keeping your word even if it really puts you out	________
• Giving in and agreeing when you are sure you are right just to 'keep the peace'	________
Asking others for favours	________
Asking for affection or consideration	________
Sticking to a decision you feel is right even if it is unpopular	________
Asking for a raise or promotion	________

Scoring

Now add up all the points. Items marked • should be reversed so you will need to subtract these points from your overall score.

How to Interpret Your Score

40-54 points	Your assertion level is excellent. You feel comfortable expressing yourself and feel in control of most situations.
13-39	You vacillate between assertive and non-assertive behaviour. Perhaps you handle some situations well but feel inhibited in others. There is room for improvement.
0-12	Your ability to communicate feelings and wishes is very poor. You are lacking in confidence, you may feel abused by others and powerless. You definitely need work to improve in this area.

Becoming More Assertive and Taking Control

Step One Recognise unassertive behaviours

Step Two Use personal assertive rights

Step Three Talk yourself into acting assertively

Step One—Recognise Unassertive Behaviours

Games people play to avoid asserting themselves

Society and families often teach us that it is not safe to come right out and say or do what we want to. You may have learnt to believe that being honest and expressing negative feelings directly will antagonise or hurt others and make you unpopular or rejected.

However, sometimes it is impossible to deny feelings completely and you may try to get what you want indirectly.

We have called these indirect patterns of behaviour unassertive games. It is useful to be aware of these games both in yourself and others, so you will have a better understanding of what is going on and therefore deal with these behaviours more effectively.

How to tell if you are being manipulated or manipulative

Unassertive people have difficulty being direct about their wishes or feelings, which means they are often very skilled at being indirect or subtle in getting what they want. Unfortunately, this indirect

SORRY, NOT TODAY. SOME OTHER TIME. THANKS, BUT NO THANKS...
NOPE. THE ANSWER IS NO. OUT OF THE QUESTION...
NOT ON YOUR LIFE! NIX! FORGET IT, PAL! NO DEAL!
I ALWAYS LIKE TO WORK OUT BEFORE A MEETING...

way of communicating or relating to others often turns into manipulation of others. Manipulation is unfair and destructive to relationships because the person who is being manipulated is often:

- unaware of it
- has no protection against it
- feels powerless
- feels angry and resentful when they realise what is happening

See if you recognise any of these methods of manipulation:

Game One—The Sufferer or After All I've Done For You

Manipulation by Guilt

When someone is the sufferer, he or she is aiming to get attention, sympathy, recognition or power from another person. The sufferers manipulate you into doing what they want by making you feel guilty. They act very self-righteously and claim, 'I'm only trying to help!', while they tell you what to do. This is their method of gaining control in your life.

The sufferer's expectation is 'because I've done things for you in the past, now you should do what I want!'. Parents often play this game with their children. The unfair advantage taken by sufferers is that you probably had no control over what they did for you. It was totally their choice. But now they are giving you no choice in what you do for them. They are making all the rules.

The disadvantage in being a sufferer is that you cause others to feel angry and resentful as well as guilty. This game therefore pushes people away from you instead of bringing them closer. The problem is that the sufferer confuses caring with behaving. Sufferers want people to show care in certain ways that they approve of. They forget that people show care in many different ways. As a result they often feel depressed and unappreciated.

Game Two—The Fence-Sitter or Whatever You Want

Manipulation by Passivity

The assumption made is that by being noncommital you will not offend anyone. When giving away your right to make a decision, you may justify it to yourself by saying 'It keeps the peace', or

'I'm only trying to keep my husband happy'. The mistaken belief in this way of thinking is that by keeping others happy your life will also be content.

Playing this game also has the advantage that you can avoid making decisions which you are not confident about. By being a fence-sitter, you force others to take control of situations and act on your behalf, when they may not wish to do so. This is how the manipulation occurs. The fence-sitter, by avoiding decisions also avoids making mistakes, and when a mistake is made, they have someone else to blame! The fence-sitter thus avoids responsibility.

When feeling down, people often let others make decisions, as they have lost confidence in their own ability to do so. This can cause resentment in others. Another disadvantage is that others take more control over your life than you may want and you find that you have less and less say in how your life is run. This results in further loss of confidence and self-esteem.

Game Three—The Wet Blanket or I Won't Disagree But I Won't Help You Either

Manipulation by Withholding Support

When people are wet blankets, they totally disagree with you but will not say so. Their game involves withholding support in an attempt to make you do what they want without directly stating this. This may be done by giving reasons for non co-operation. If questioned, wet blankets usually come up with yet another excuse for their behaviour. Wet blankets are very good at pointing out all the flaws in your plan without offering any positive suggestions or real help. Furthermore, they tend not to be available when you need them.

This game often causes others to feel let down, hurt and angry. It has a damaging effect on trust in a relationship.

By not giving support or encouragement, wet blankets hope to win others around to their way of thinking by wearing down their enthusiasm. They also hope that others will guess their real feelings so they can avoid stating them directly.

Game Four—The Spoilsport or I'll Appear To Go Along, But If I Can't Have What I Want, I'll Spoil It For You Too

Manipulation by Destroying Pleasure

Spoilsports hate not getting their own way so much that they cannot bear others to be happy while they are angry. To avoid conflict they go along with everyone but really feel angry and resentful. Their annoyance is usually expressed by repeated complaints or criticism, which results in others feeling as annoyed as they are! They may be annoyed because their opinion was not sought out or adhered to. Spoilsports want people to show more consideration for their feelings. Unfortunately, because they are so often complaining, people are reluctant to be considerate towards them.

These are some of the more common unassertive games. There are many others. If you recognise these behaviours in yourself, then read on!

Step Two—Using Your Personal Rights

The following is a list of personal rights available to everyone in our society. Read through this list and note how many of these rights you are currently using. If you are not allowing yourself these rights then you need to begin using them. Are you giving these rights to other people and not to yourself? Perhaps, as is common with unassertive people, you are not allowing yourself or others these rights?

Bill of Assertive Rights

- You have the right to your own values; other people have a right to their values.
- You have the right to feel and express your feelings, including anger; other people have the right to express their feelings.
- You have the right to offer no reasons and excuses for your behaviour; other people have the right not to explain themselves.
- You have the right to make mistakes and be responsible for them; others have the right to make mistakes and accept the consequences.

- You have the right to change your mind; others have the right to change their minds.
- You have the right to make your own decisions; other people have the right to make their own decisions.
- You have the right to say: I don't know or I don't care or I don't understand; other people have these rights also.
- You have the right to praise yourself and feel good; others have the right to praise themselves.
- You have the right to say no without feeling guilty or selfish; others have the right to say no to you without being considered selfish.
- You have the right to use your time in ways you choose; others have the right to use their time in their way.
- You have the right to ask for affection, help or information; other people have the right to ask for these things.

EXERCISE 17

If you find that you are not using all your personal rights, nominate ones to work on as weekly goals. You may find it useful to pin up these rights somewhere in your home or office as a reminder.

Step Three—Talk Yourself Into Assertion

Negative thinking causes a block to assertive behaviour. It produces many unreasonable fears, which, if not examined, block communication and cause poor self-esteem.

Faulty Thinking That Blocks Assertion

1 Assuming that you know how others will react:
'He'll be upset if I say . . .',
'She'll think I'm cheap'.

2 Putting negative labels on assertive behaviour:
'It's bad manners',
'It's selfish or petty to mention this'.

3 Exaggerating the possible unpleasant consequences:
'I'll be horribly embarrassed',
'He'll never forgive me'.

4 Assuming that the worst will automatically happen:
'I'll lose my job if I disagree with my boss'.

5 Setting limiting restrictions on when to be assertive:
'I'll only say it if the time is right',
'The other person must be able to handle it',
'I must be 100 per cent sure of my facts'.

6 Talking yourself out of how you really feel is called 'rationalising':
'I don't really mind that much', when you really do mind! or
'He's only saying that for my own good, I shouldn't complain'.

7 Talking yourself out of the responsibility for assertive action:
'It'll all work out in the end' or
'It's not my fault, someone else should do something' or
'I couldn't change things anyhow'.

8 Believing that your strong feelings are automatically right and others are wrong. This is emotional reasoning which means that you believe feelings are facts. For example:
'I feel put down, therefore I was'.
This type of thinking encourages aggressive behaviour.

9 Having unrealistic expectations about the outcome of assertive behaviour. You may expect that by being assertive all your problems will be solved. Some people expect that assertion will work the first time, or that others will always co-operate if they are assertive. This can result in them giving up if the first attempt was unsuccessful. Assertion is not a magic wand which works all the time. However, it does improve your chances of getting what you want, even though it does not guarantee success!

10 Taking too much responsibility for another person's feelings. This means that you blame yourself if someone gets angry, upset or hurt as a result of you being assertive. If you have been reasonable, rational and non-aggressive, it is not your fault if the other person overreacts! How another person reacts to your assertiveness is determined by their thinking style. This is something over which you have no control. The way someone else interprets your behaviour is the result of their early conditioning. If they are behaving irrationally, then it is their responsibility to correct their own behaviour and thinking. If you allow other people's overreactions to stop you from being assertive, you are doing both yourself and them a disservice. By giving in to irrational behaviour, you are giving an impression that it is reasonable.

Talking Yourself Into Assertive Behaviour—Challenge Your Fears

By analysing your thinking systematically in situations that require assertive behaviour, you will become aware of specific fears that are blocking you.

The Fear of Making a Mistake

To challenge this fear, ask yourself the following questions:

- Are you overemphasising the significance of making a mistake?
- Are you assuming that others will think the worst of you without any evidence for this?
- Do you tend to put others down just because they made a mistake?
- What can you do to correct or minimise your mistake?

The Fear of Rejection

This is often a block to assertion. See Chapter 8 for tips in overcoming this fear.

Assuming Negative Reactions to Your Assertiveness

Where is your evidence that your thinking is correct?
If the worst did happen are there ways you might handle it?
What can you do to deal with an unpleasant reaction to your assertive behaviour?

Managing Anger

Intense anger, like anxiety and depression, is often caused by illogical thinking that distorts the event. Accepting the cognitive premise that you create your feelings by your thoughts means you must take responsibility for your anger. Now anger is not a dirty word. It is an energising emotion which will encourage you to make changes, if you let it!

Whether you are able to use anger productively or destructively depends on your thinking style and your manner of communication. Anger, like depression, gives you the choice of either changing yourself (this means your attitudes and behaviour), or changing your predicament (this may mean the way you are treated by others).

When managing anger do not assume that there is a good reason for it! Many people believe that because they feel angry, they have been wronged. What if your anger has been created solely by your illogical thoughts?

Anger, to be most effective, needs to be expressed at the time it occurs. This gets things off your chest before they build up. You also have an improved likelihood of making an immediate change in things you are unhappy about.

Substitute Realistic Thoughts to Encourage Assertion

Once you have examined and challenged fears that block assertion, talk to yourself rationally to encourage new assertive behaviour. Here are some examples:

> It's OK for me to speak up even if I'm not completely sure of my facts. This way I'll find out what others think of my idea.
>
> He may not like hearing what I am going to say. I can accept that. His anger doesn't have to upset me. There's every chance he will calm down eventually. I can wait.
>
> It is important for me to say something as her behaviour has been annoying me. If she gets upset as I think she will, I don't need to feel guilty because I am being reasonable. How she reacts is largely out of my control.
>
> I can show that I care for her feelings without backing down.
>
> I can practise dealing with difficult situations and not deny my anger. I will get useful practise in dealing with things I don't like.

Validate Yourself

Remind yourself that you matter and that your feelings and rights are as important as those of other people. It helps to tell yourself that feelings are not necessarily wrong or right—they just exist! You have the right to let people know your feelings and ask that they be respected.

If you are confused or unsure about how you really feel, it is reasonable to say something like: 'I'm not sure how I feel about that right now. I want some time to think and then I'll let you know.' You do not have to give someone an instant answer just because that is what they want!

Once again it is important that you analyse your thinking to be sure that it is realistic. If your thinking is distorted then your feelings or requests may be inappropriate. This in turn reduces the chances of co-operation by others.

Use Your Personal Assertive Rights

Do you tend to treat other people better than yourself? If you give others, but not yourself, the right to say no, or to break commitments, then you are setting yourself up to feel exploited. Remind yourself of the particular right you may be practising before and during the situation.

Check That Your Expectations are Reasonable

These expectations relate to both your own and other people's behaviour. There is a good chance that you will feel disappointed in yourself if expectations of your own behaviour sound something like this:

> I must do it perfectly.
> I must be assertive without getting upset.
> I will always be assertive from now on.

Similarly, you may find that you feel let down if your expectations are not lived up to and sound like this:

> They must respect my feelings always.
> She should not be upset by what I said.
> I shouldn't have to repeat myself.

Simply being assertive does not guarantee that other people will respect your feelings. We do not live in a perfect world. If others react aggressively or irrationally to your assertiveness, then it is most important that you do not automatically blame yourself or put yourself down! Other people's reactions will be caused by their own thinking styles which are out of your control. Accept their feelings as well as your own and agree to disagree. Remember, they may see things differently when they calm down. By approaching a situation assertively, you know that you have made a reasonable attempt to deal with the problem. This is important for your self-confidence.

Set Assertiveness Tasks

To encourage behaviour change, decide on daily and weekly exercises in assertion. Choose easy situations to start practising your assertiveness and build up to more difficult ones.

Plan and rehearse what you want to say and do. Write it out beforehand and learn it if you feel anxiety will make you go blank in the situation.

The key to being assertive is to be consistent and persistent. If you try just once and give up or give in, you are simply teaching people that you will back down eventually. This will make them try harder to get their way. By being firm and sticking to your point, you are giving the message that they must change.

This chapter is intended as an introduction and overview of the area of assertion and its relationship to depression. There are many more skills under the general heading of assertion that we have not covered here. If you feel that you require more understanding and training in assertion, then we suggest that you contact a psychologist who conducts training programmes in assertion and communication skills. If you wish to do further reading in this area, we have included a list of useful books in the reading list at the end of the book.

Chapter 10

HOW TO LIVE WITH SOMEONE WHO IS DEPRESSED: A CHAPTER FOR FAMILIES

'He is a man who is impossible to please because he is never pleased with himself.'

GOETHE

A book of this nature would not be complete without a chapter for the family members supporting someone who is depressed. The plight of such families can be a very difficult and confusing one. The messages which the family receives may be hurtful and inconsistent, sometimes suggesting blame and hostility and at other times dependency and despair. As a close friend or relative of someone who is feeling depressed, you may be told:

Help me—but stay away.
I need you—but what I'm going through is all your fault.

It is, therefore, not surprising that many families struggle to deal with the distressing time which they are undergoing. As shown throughout this book, if depression is to be overcome, negative and unhelpful attitudes and reactions need to change. In line with this, there are certain things which family members and friends can do to help the person experiencing depression towards recovery. This chapter includes a range of techniques which will equip you to deal more easily with the depression which is affecting your family.

Depression and the Family

Sometimes it is difficult at first to accept that someone close to you is suffering from depression. The initial hurdle to overcome is that of accepting both the condition and its effects on you. Then you can stop pulling against the effects of the depression and begin to work constructively and positively to help the sufferer. Family and friends often go through the following stages on the way:

Disregarding the signs In the early stage you may play down and disregard the changes in your relative or friend's behaviour. You may even think that you are imagining the changes.

Rationalising As you become more aware of the depression, you may attempt to account for it. This often involves rationalisations such as:

It's probably a viral illness and she'll get over it in a day or so.
He's just tired.
She is long overdue for a holiday

Denial When you realise that the person has not returned to normal, shock and denial are frequent reactions which may be conveyed by such comments as:

No one in our family has been depressed like this before; these things just don't happen to us.

Guilt Once the extent of the mood change is realised, there is often a time of searching for the cause of the depression. During this phase the family may go through a period of blame and guilt. You may assume that you are to blame and ask:

Where did we go wrong?
If only we had done such and such this would never have happened.

Although it may be useful to seek the cause of the depression for a short period of time, families should not fall into the trap of blaming themselves, particular events, the depressed person or someone else! Blaming someone is a negative reaction in dealing with the problem of depression. It tends to oversimplify the cause and effect, which is not useful, as depression is a complex problem. You cannot undo what has happened in the past, so why dwell on it? To do so is a waste of time and energy and can make you feel worse.

Blaming yourself leads to feelings of guilt and actions and decisions which are based on guilt are not usually productive. Some people who are guilt-ridden become overly involved, and try to compensate for what they perceive they did to bring on the depression. Others cope with guilt by detaching themselves from the person so as to avoid being reminded of their distressed feelings. They may do this, for instance, by refusing to visit the person in hospital while he is feeling depressed.

Anger There is often a stage when you feel frustrated and angry. At times these feelings are directed towards the person who is experiencing the depression, and expressed as:

Why are you doing this to us?
Just pull your socks up and get on with it.
We've had enough of your moods.

To help your relative or friend deal with the depression, examine what is happening in the present. How do you behave towards the person when he is feeling down? Are you maintaining a balance between showing the person that you are genuinely concerned for him on the one hand, and giving him responsibility for his own thoughts, feelings and behaviours on the other?

For example, if a person has money problems, try exploring options for raising finances in the short-term and developing more financial security in the long-term. Simply offering to pay the debts each time will not do anything for self-confidence, budgeting skills or coping strategies.

Respect for a person who is feeling depressed means being encouraging and supportive, but firm in helping him to do things for himself. This can be a delicate balance to maintain. Sometimes families swing one way or the other, either pampering the person while he is down, or rejecting him. If the family makes all decisions on behalf of the person feeling depressed, then this encourages him to remain passive and helpless. He may even feel trapped in this victim role as he feels that his independence is slipping away. This can lead to a belief that he has no control over what happens in his life.

The family can help in the following ways:

Validate the Person's Feelings

Many depressed people believe that their family, friends and work colleagues do not really understand what they are going through and they are probably right. Unless you have been depressed, it is difficult to understand how it feels. Nevertheless, the family can do certain things to help the person feel cared for. A good start is to accept that the person is suffering from emotional pain. Do not belittle it or question whether it is real or not. Even if you cannot understand why he is depressed, just try to accept that it is happening, whatever the reason.

Relate to the Person—Not Their Depression

Depression is only a part of that person's experience. The person does not become his depression. Try to ensure that you talk to him as a person with a specific problem, that of a set of symptoms and signs which we refer to as the depression. In doing so you are separating the problem from the person. The benefit in doing this is that you can then empathise with him as to how frustrating it must be to put up with. When you are angry, you can let him know that it is the depression that you are fed up with and not him as a person.

Communicate Effectively

By using effective listening and communication skills, family members can help the person feeling down to express her needs and feelings. Taking a few minutes to try to put yourself in her shoes can reduce your impulse to become impatient or irritable. Show a genuine interest in what she is saying and give her a chance to finish without interrupting. If you have effective listening skills you are less likely to misinterpret what she is trying to say, or to jump to conclusions. Here are some techniques which can help you:

- **Empathic Statements** Show that you are trying to understand. By letting the person know that you are listening and concerned, you are allowing her to open up to you. Empathy shows that you are tuning in to her feelings and experiences. Here is an example of an empathic statement:

  PETER: I can't be bothered doing anything anymore.
  MOTHER: You are having a really hard time, aren't you?

- **Taking Responsibility For Your Own Feelings** To communicate effectively you must recognise your feelings and take responsibility for them. After all, your thoughts about what the depressed person is doing cause you to feel and react in certain ways. Owning your feelings is achieved through 'I' statements. These

are messages that start with the word 'I', such as 'I feel angry when you do that'. 'I' statements are useful for letting the person know what effect his behaviour is having on you. Allowing him to understand your feelings will help avoid misunderstandings and unnecessary conflict.

On the other hand, 'you' statements, such as 'You make me angry', serve to put responsibility for the way you are feeling onto the other person. Statements like this imply that you are blaming the depressed person for your feelings which will lead him to greater demoralisation and loss of self-esteem. Furthermore, such statements are aggressive and tend to make the other person defensive and less likely to listen to you.

- **Being Direct** Indirect ways of communicating often involve manipulation of others, which is generally destructive of relationships. Chapter 9 gives examples of such patterns. Relationships amongst family members are strengthened by discussion and negotiation, rather than indirect messages.

For example, Ruth was feeling anxious about being alone and wanted her daughter to visit more often. Trying to get her daughter to visit by complaining about her health would be an indirect way of expressing this desire. On the other hand, if Ruth asked for help specifically and directly, her daughter is in a better position to understand her mother's needs and to help her deal with them.

The family members also need to be direct about their individual needs. For example:

I would like to get out of the house this week-end.
I need a short break. I would like to see some friends.
I would like you to come along, even if you don't feel the best.

- **Reflecting Feelings** When people are feeling distressed, what they say may not be an accurate reflection of how they feel. It is, therefore, useful to feed back the feelings that are being expressed (as they seem to you), rather than the content. What the person is saying is the content and how they are saying it suggests the feeling. This is a good way to lead into it:

You sound . . . (upset, angry, hurt).

David (to his wife): My boss should have consulted me before going ahead with the plan. He must not think much of my judgement.

David's wife (reflecting feelings): You sound hurt.

It can then prove useful to ask the person if they would like to talk about it further.

David's wife: Tell me more about it. It may make you feel better if you get it off your chest.

When his wife communicates in this way, David is more likely to feel that she is really making an effort to understand. It may be that David does not want to talk about the matter further and his wife should respect this. Nevertheless, she has given him a clear message that she is interested, concerned and available.

Give Positive Messages

When a person is depressed, reassure her that she is loved and has a valuable part to play in the family. You can do this by frequent positive messages. Examples may include:

It's good to be here with you.
You chose a great shirt.
I'm pleased that you came along.

We all thrive on feedback. It helps us to monitor and reflect on our own behaviour. It is especially significant for people who are depressed, as they often lose their confidence in making decisions and so rely more on the comments and judgements of others. The most useful feedback involves commenting positively on what the person has managed to do and not what she did not do. To do this it may be necessary to look for small changes which have been made, if major changes are not obvious. Look for signs of effort and praise these. The depressed person's awareness of positive changes are the building blocks for restoring self-confidence. Examples:

I liked the way you handled that . . . (be specific).
It must have been difficult for you to have done that while feeling down. It's good that you had a go.

How to Help With Decision-Making

It is best to avoid directly advising a person who is depressed on what he should do. Instead, ask him what he thinks his options or choices are. Look for the positives in what has already been done and help him to reach his own solutions. In doing so, you are helping him to realise that there are choices available for him (even doing nothing is a choice). You are also giving an important positive message that you believe him to be capable of making decisions and taking responsibility. You should respect the decisions he makes even if you do not agree, or have a better one yourself.

Clarify How You Help Most Effectively

It can be very confusing when a person is depressed to know what will be helpful. As this is different for each person you really need to check it out directly. A good time to do this is when the person is feeling reasonably well. Discuss with her in specific terms what she would find helpful if she becomes down again in the future.

Michelle asked her parents to continue to organise activities that included her, even if she did not feel particularly like being involved. Having their encouragement to participate helped her to reverse her slide into isolation and withdrawn behaviour which always made her feel much worse.

Ruth felt at one stage that her family and friends were putting pressure on her when they frequently asked her how she was feeling. She asked them not to enquire about her health so often as she did not wish to think and talk about it constantly. She told them that she cheered up when the conversation was about issues that distracted her from her negative thoughts.

Katherine became upset when her family persisted in reminding her how confident, practical and capable she used to be before she felt depressed. This tended to set off a series of negative thoughts which made her feel even more inadequate. She asked her family to stop making comparisons with her past behaviour and instead to compliment her on the tasks which she was able to perform now.

How To Ask a Person Who is Feeling Depressed to Change His Behaviour

In every family there are members who develop mannerisms which the others find irritating. Running late, slurping soup, interrupting and nagging are some common bad habits. It is understandable that families may feel reticent about raising these issues with the depressed person, fearing that it may cause further distress. However, not communicating your concerns can have detrimental effects. When feelings are bottled up, they tend to come out in indirect ways which are not relevant to the real problem. This is often seen when people dwell on trivial matters as a way of avoiding bigger problems.

A technique is described below which is most effective for requesting that a person change his behaviour in a particular way. This technique devised by Bower & Bower[1] has four stages:

(i) **Describe** the behaviour which you wish to be changed, briefly and objectively. It is best to refer to a specific example of the behaviour, rather than generalising. Imagine yourself to be a scientific observer instead of someone who is emotionally involved. State when the behaviour took place, how many times it occurred and what it was:

> When we were having dinner with our friends tonight, you interrupted me on four occasions and finished my sentences for me.

Avoid statements such as 'You are always doing . . . (such and such)'. If you use emotionally loaded words, you may well end up with an argument. Also avoid judging the behaviour as selfishness, and offer a description of what happened.

(ii) **Express** how you felt at the time. Make sure that you take responsibility for how you felt by using an 'I' statement (I felt angry), rather than a 'you' statement (You made me angry). Accusing someone of making you feel something, is aggressive. 'I felt annoyed when we were out this evening', is an example of an 'I' statement.

(iii) **Specify** what you would prefer the person to do. By giving a clear alternative, he is more likely to understand how to deal with the situation differently. For example,

> I'd appreciate it if you waited until I have finished talking and then I'd like to hear what you have to say.

Requests such as 'I wish you would be more considerate', are too vague and not very helpful. Spell out clearly and specifically how you would like them to behave.

(iv) **Comment on Consequence**—how things would be better for you both if the person changed this behaviour. Again, it is important that it is couched in positive terms. For example:

> If you did this I'm sure that we would both enjoy the evening more.

Here is an example of this technique in action:

David's wife found it frustrating when he indicated that he intended to go out with her and right at the last minute, he would change his mind. She used the following steps just described to discuss her concerns with David.

DESCRIBE—	David, twice this week-end we have been about to go out and you have changed your mind just before going.
EXPRESS—	I feel disappointed and frustrated when you do this.
SPECIFY—	I'd like you to come out when you've said you would.
CONSEQUENCE—	We would then look forward to doing things together. Going out may also make you feel better.

This technique can be used for a variety of purposes. Use it as the basis of a letter, a telephone conversation or face-to-face discussion.

Eliminate Unhelpful Family Expectations

Every family functions as a system and so a problem faced by one person will have some effect on everyone else in the family. Fundamental to the system's functioning is a set of expectations specific to that particular family. Your family may or may not be aware of the precise nature of these rules and expectations which may be helpful:

> We should stick together in difficult times.
>
> It does not matter what you do, we will still love you.

Family expectations can also be unhelpful and may actually contribute to maintaining the depression of a family member.

> You should never discuss or show unpleasant feelings.
>
> Unless you are outstanding in your performances, we will be disappointed in you.
>
> To show any weakness is a sign of failure as a person.
>
> The males in our family are strong and the females are weak.

Attempting to live by these expectations may cause distress. Look closely at the expectations held in your family and consider whether they are helpful. It is important for families to be flexible and not to adhere to fixed rules which are causing distress. A family therapist may be able to help with these issues.

Establish Your Own Supports

Providing support for a person who is feeling depressed can be demanding both physically and emotionally. David's wife describes some of the stresses the family experiences at this time:

> When David is feeling really bad with the depression it affects everyone in the family in different ways. Our youngest boy becomes angry towards

David, which is probably his way of showing he is confused and frightened. Our eldest son tends to withdraw and stays in his room. I try to spend more time with David to see if he wants to talk, but I sometimes get so frustrated. Our conversations tend to go round in circles and he often repeats the same thing over and over. I get a strange feeling that I've been through this all before. The whole process seems so energy-consuming, so irritating, so futile. Sometimes I get a compelling need to get away and be in touch with normality again and to escape the situation at any cost.

As a support person, it is essential that you give some time to yourself to pursue your own needs and interests. It is a myth that you must always be loving and caring. Feelings of anger and frustration are normal and common reactions to a difficult situation. It is helpful if you can discuss such feelings with someone other than the person who is feeling depressed. If you do not do this you may well feel resentful and guilty that you were angry.

You need breaks and your own sources of emotional support in order to be an effective support. Do not feel guilty for giving yourself time out to enjoy yourself.

What To Do if Someone in Your Family is Feeling Suicidal

Thoughts of suicide are commonly experienced by people when they are depressed. Intentions to suicide with specific plans are less common and more serious. There are various things that family and friends can do to help during this distressing and difficult time.

Talk to the Person About His Suicidal Thoughts and Intentions

If you suspect that someone you know is thinking about suicide then ask directly, 'Have you thought of harming yourself or taking your life?'. There is a taboo in our society about asking such direct questions which is probably based on a fear of dealing with the responses. It is generally a relief for the person who is distressed to share his feelings. You can help by listening and encouraging him to talk about his overwhelming sense of hopelessness.

Validate His Feelings

Accept the feelings for what they are and discuss suicide as a possibility rather than an unthinkable idea. To imply that the person is wrong or silly to feel this way or to judge and condemn him would probably inhibit him from opening up to you in the future. Such thoughts are often a plea for help and a desperate attempt to escape from problems and distressing feelings.

Identify His Fears

Try to encourage the person to be specific about what is troubling him. When people are depressed, they tend to view their problems in global ways and make extremely critical judgements such as 'My whole life is a failure'. By discussing specific problems you can help the person work out ways of dealing with the hurdles that seem insurmountable. It is important to dispute the idea that suicide is the best or most viable solution to the problem.

Investigate the Consequences

Encourage the person to consider the consequences of suiciding, especially the effect it may have on the people he cares about.

Differentiate Between Suicidal Thoughts and Intentions

Establish whether the person has vague suicidal notions such as 'What's the point', 'I can't be bothered going on', as opposed to definite plans and intentions to take his life. Ask him specifically what he is contemplating. It may then be necessary to remove tablets or guns from the house.

Stay With the Person

If the person has suicidal intentions, try not to let him be alone for long periods. Rather than watch over him in an overly vigilant way, it is better to check where he is every 15 minutes or so. If you watch over him too closely then he may isolate himself or feel that you do not trust him. This is a short-term measure (for hours only) and you should not feel obliged to continue for longer periods.

However, you should realise that if someone is determined to take his life, there may be little you can do to stop him. It is ultimately his responsibility to make this choice and you must not think that it is up to you to stop him from doing so.

Encourage Him to Seek Professional Help

Even severe depressions are treatable, so encourage the person to seek professional help immediately. Contact your family doctor to arrange the appropriate treatment. If professional help is refused, suggest that the depressed person talk to someone else he respects.

What To Do After a Suicide Attempt

If someone close to you survives a suicide attempt, talk about the issues that led to the attempt when he is ready. For instance, if it was the result of low self-esteem following the break-up of a relationship, you can help by giving positive messages to improve his feelings of self-worth. Tell the person how much he means to you. Promote social contact with other people so that he is not too dependent on one relationship.

Often intense feelings of anger are experienced by people who attempt suicide. If this is the case, it may be necessary for you to encourage and accept their expressions of anger. This may be difficult if one of the family rules is that anger should not be directly expressed. It may also be useful to investigate the myths held by the depressed person regarding the expression of angry feelings. Sometimes people believe that others will reject them if they show their anger. Other people fear losing control. Encouraging more effective strategies for expressing emotions will mean less likelihood of feelings being acted out in indirect ways, such as suicide attempts.

Repeated Suicide Threats

Sometimes suicide threats are a distressed person's way of eliciting help and sympathy or of avoiding conflict. If repeated suicide threats occur, that person must learn other strategies for getting his needs met. Rather than focusing on the suicide threats, investigate the underlying problem. If the suicide threat is permitted to become a problem in itself, it will distract attention from the real issues.

Family Reactions to Suicide Attempts

When a person attempts to take his life, the family goes through many emotions. You may initially be in shock and be unable to believe what has happened. Anger is a common reaction and this is sometimes directed at health professionals. Guilt occurs if families believe that they could have done something to prevent the incident.

Fundamental philosophical beliefs about life may be shaken when someone you are close to attempts or commits suicide. When faced with the self-destructiveness of this event, families often experience times of introspection and fear. This fear may be about their own death and the fragility of life.

Meeting Your Own Needs

If you feel unable to deal with the person's suicidal threats or attempts, or he will not allow you to talk with him, you should discuss the situation and your feelings with someone else. It is important that you deal with your own needs and feelings. If someone you care about takes his life, it may take some time to work through the multitude of feelings that occur as a result. You will get through it and you can continue to enjoy your life.

Chapter 11

SEEKING PROFESSIONAL HELP

ALICE:	*'Would you tell me please which way I ought to go from here?'*
CAT:	*'That depends a good deal on where you want to get to.'*

LEWIS CARROLL

When to Seek Professional Help

If you would like more guidance in learning the techniques in this book, then see a therapist who can work through the steps with you.

Professional help should also be sought if your depression is severe, or if you experience significant mood changes.

Biological depressions, such as manic-depressive illness, generally respond well to medication.

Suicidal thoughts and intentions are serious. If you are feeling this way, talk to someone about your distress and look at other options.

When reading this book, you may discover that your depression is associated with specific problems in your life, such as marital or assertion difficulties. Specific therapies are available to help with these issues.

Some people refuse to seek treatment for depression even if it is warranted. The usual reasons for this are:

- uncertainty of what the problem is
- fear of what may be involved in the treatment
- anxiety regarding the stigma sometimes associated with having an emotional problem
- fear of disappointing or upsetting a relationship
- fear of the reactions of others if they found out about your depression

DOCTOR, I THINK I'M DEPRESSED...
TRY TO BE MORE POSITIVE!
VERY WELL. I KNOW I'M DEPRESSED!

- a belief that 'This can't happen to me'
- becoming so familiar with the depression that you fail to realise how much it is controlling you
- mis-attributing your symptoms to an illness or to tiredness

Recognise that it is your responsibility to seek treatment when it is necessary. The longer you delay, the more difficult it will be to break the habits associated with depression.

There are both biological and psychological approaches to the treatment of depression and it may set your mind at rest to know a little more about each.

Psychological Approaches

Psychological approaches focus on developing problem solving and coping strategies and/or insight which will enable you to deal with stressful situations. Psychological treatments also look at the interpersonal issues which may be contributing to your depression.

There are several different types of psychological therapy (or psychotherapy) available. Each conceptualises depression differently and adopts varying styles of intervention.

Behaviour Therapy looks at how you structure everyday activities so that you receive more reinforcement from what you do. Your role in therapy is an active one. You learn how to control your feelings and to alter your patterns of relating to others. Cognitive (Behaviour) Therapy encompasses behavioural techniques such as self-monitoring and also extends further into the role cognitions play in determining feelings.

Assertion Training involves the mastery of communication and self-expression skills. It teaches you to become aware of what you want in a situation and to express your needs and feelings more directly. Anxiety often functions as a barrier to acting assertively and strategies for lessening anxiety are taught.

Psychoanalytic Psychotherapy emphasises the unconscious processes of the mind. It explores conflicts, feelings and fantasies associated with early childhood and other experiences. Therapy is often conducted for several years with sessions at least once each week.

Marital and Family Therapy considers the effects of depression on other members of the family and looks at patterns of relating.

In additon to individual therapy, group programmes are available for treating depression. Discussing your feelings and concerns with others can be a valuable experience.

Biological Approaches

Medical approaches understand depression as an illness and the subsequent treatments aim to reduce or get rid of the symptoms of the depression.

Antidepressant medications: The three most common types of antidepressants are tricyclics, monoamine oxidase inhibitors (MAOIs) and lithium carbonate. These medications are used to correct the neurotransmitter disturbances associated with biological depressions. Usually it takes three weeks to obtain a therapeutic effect. Antidepressants may cause side-effects including a dry mouth, constipation, drowsiness, difficulty in focusing and shakiness. For these reasons medications are often used for short periods only.

Using psychotherapy for the treatment of your depression does not mean that you cannot have some recourse to antidepressant medications. Medication can be useful to relieve distressing experiences, especially if your depression is biological in nature. However, medication does not change the stresses and social factors which triggered your depression in the first place. It is, therefore, a good practice to learn how to protect yourself from distressing emotions and reduce your dependency on medications.

Electro-convulsive Therapy (ECT) ECT was introduced as a treatment for mental illness in the 1930s. In the early days it was crude and gained a poor reputation. Its use has been significantly refined over the years and its safety has improved. Confusion and memory problems are often experienced immediately after ECT, but these side-effects as a rule are fully reversible after a couple of weeks. When used carefully and sparingly, ECT has a role to play in the treatment of biological depressions.

Choosing a Therapist

Qualified clinical psychologists specialise in providing psychotherapy. Over the decades psychologists have received considerable recognition in their pioneering work, especially in Cognitive Therapy and other Behavioural Therapies. Unlike psychiatrists, psychologists are not qualified to administer medications, so emphasis has traditionally focused on coping strategies.

Locating a therapist: Clinical Psychologists are located at community clinics, hospitals and in private practice. The telephone book can be a useful guide to find the closest clinical psychologist to you. It is best in the early stage to obtain the names of several psychologists. You can then contact each of the therapists and enquire specifically about their particular approaches.

What to do if you find that therapy is not working:

- Talk it over with your therapist
- Examine your expectations
- Consider whether this particular approach is best suited to your particular needs
- Most importantly, don't give up!

Conclusion

Ultimately, getting better is in your hands. You can control what you think and therefore how you feel. By changing the pattern of your beliefs, you can gain more control over your life. It is an exciting experience when you realise that you have the power over your own destiny. This can give you the opportunity and hope for a new perspective and a more adaptive philosophy of life.

> 'You are the creator of your own universe.
> For as a human being you are free to will whatever state of being you desire,
> Through the use of your thoughts and words there is great power there.
> It can be a blessing or a curse,
> It is entirely up to you.
> For the quality of your life is brought about by the quality of your thinking.
> Think about that!'

CLARK, ST. JOHN-CHRISTIE Theme from *Time.*[1]

APPENDIX

How Effective is Cognitive Therapy?

Cognitive Therapy has become recognised throughout the world as a highly successful form of treatment for disabling, distressing and persistent feelings of depression, anxiety and anger. The application of Cognitive Therapy to depression was made popular by Aaron Beck. A growing body of research has supported the effectiveness of this approach and its popularity has flourished. A series of studies were conducted by Beck and his eminent colleagues in Pennsylvania. In one of their studies,[1] they compared Cognitive Therapy with Tofranil (a widely used antidepressant medication) over a 12 week period. Forty severely depressed people were randomly assigned to one of the two groups. Not only did Cognitive Therapy work at least as well as drug treatment for certain presentations of depression, it also appeared to have more lasting effects. Recent research suggests that the relapse rate is significantly reduced if people become skilful in self-control techniques instead of relying solely on medication.

Our personal experience also testifies to the clinical success of Cognitive Therapy. We have spent many years treating various depressions and anxieties. Many people referred to us for Cognitive Therapy were not responding to medication or other psychotherapeutic approaches. Many had experienced moderate to severe depression for months and sometimes years. Some felt hopeless about recovery and had come to us as a last resort. Depression had become a way of life for them.

Our results using Cognitive Therapy have been extremely encouraging. Most people who have completed therapy, which we conduct both individually and in groups, have described a significant reduction in their symptoms. Some claim to be feeling the best they have for years. Others have described a sense of relief as they look at their lives in a new way and put their problems in a new perspective.

NOTES AND REFERENCES

Introduction

1 Seligman, M.E.P. *Helplessness*, San Francisco, Freeman, 1975.

2 Beck, A.T. *Cognitive Therapy and the Emotional Disorders*, New York, New American Library, 1976.

3 Ellis, Albert and Robert Harper *A New Guide to Rational Living*, Hollywood, Wilshire Book Company, 1975.

4 Burns, D.D. *Feeling Good—The New Mood Therapy*, New York, New American Library, 1980.

Chapter 1

EXERCISE 1: Boyce P.M. 'Visual Analogue Scale For Depression, Consultant Psychiatrist, Mood Disorders Clinic, Prince Henry Hospital, Sydney, 1987.

Chapter 2

1 Boyce, P.M. 'Depression and the Life Cycle', *Patient Management*, September, 1986, pp 69-77.

EXERCISE 2: Boyce, P.M. and Parker, G. 'Development of a Scale to Measure Interpersonal Sensitivity', *Australian and New Zealand Journal of Psychiatry*, 1989 (in press).

EXERCISE 3: Tennant, C. and Andrews, G. 'A Scale To Measure The Stress Of Life Events', *Australian and New Zealand Journal of Psychiatry*, 1976, 10, pp 27-32.

Chapter 3

EXERCISE 4: Hollon, S.D. and Kendall, T.C. 'Cognitive Self-Statements in Depression: Development of an Automatic Thoughts Questionnaire', *Cognitive Therapy and Research*, 1980.

EXERCISE 5: Wilson, P. 'The Daily Mood Monitor', Lecturer in Psychology, Psychology Department, University of Sydney, 1987.

Chapter 4

1 Burns, D.D. *Feeling Good—The New Mood Therapy*, New York, The New American Library, 1980.

2 Beck A.T., Rush, A.J., Shaw, B.F. and Emery, G. *Cognitive Therapy of Depression: A Treatment Manual*, New York, Guilford, 1979.

Chapter 8

1 Satir, V. *Peoplemaking*, Palo Alto, CA, Science and Behaviour Books, 1972.

2 and 3 Burns, D.D. *Feeling Good—The New Mood Therapy*, New York, The New American Library, 1980.

Chapter 9

Alberti, Robert E. and Emmons, Michael L. *Your Perfect Right*, California, Impact Publishers, 1978.

Bower, Sharon Anthony and Bower, Gordon H. *Asserting Your Self*, Massachusetts, Addison-Wesley Publishing Company, 1984.

Dickson, Anne, *A Woman in Your Own Right*, London, Quartet Books, 1982.

Dyer, Dr. Wayne W. *Pulling Your Own Strings*, New York, Avon, 1979.

Fensterheim, Herbert and Baer, Jean *Don't Say 'Yes' When You Want To Say 'No'*, London, Futura Macdonald & Co., 1976.

Chapter 10

1 Bower, S.A. and Bower, G.H. Asserting Yourself: *A Positive Guide for Positive Change*, Massachusetts, Addison Wesley, 1980.

Chapter 11

1 Extract from Dave Clark's *Time the Musical* © 1986 Spurs Music Publishing Limited, 12 Thayer Street, London W1M 6AU.

Appendix A

1 Beck, A.T., Rush, A.J., Shaw, B.F. and Emery, G. *Cognitive Therapy of Depression*, New York, Guilford Press, 1979.

FURTHER READING

Depression

Burns, D.D. *Feeling Good—The New Mood Therapy*, New York, New American Library, 1980.

Lewinsohn, P.M., Munoz, R.F., Youngren, M.A. and Zeiss, A.M. *Control Your Depression*, New York, Prentice Hall Press.

Rowe, D. Depression—*The Way Out of Your Prison*, London, Routledge and Kegan Paul, 1983.

Rush, J. *Beating Depression*, London, Century Publishing, 1983.

Self Esteem

McKay, M. and Fanning, P. Self-Esteem—*A Proven Programme of Cognitive Techniques for Assessing, Improving, and Maintaining Self Esteem*, California, New Harbinger Publications, 1987.

Relationships

Biddulph, S. and S. *The Making of Love*, Sydney, Doubleday, 1988.

Montgomery, B. & Evans, L. *Living and Loving Together*, Melbourne, Nelson, 1987.

Norwood, R. *Women Who Love Too Much*, London, Arrow Books, 1988.

Families

Skynner, R. and Cleese, J. *Families and How to Survive Them*, London, Methuen, 1985.

Stress

Montgomery, B. and Evans, L. *You and Stress—A Guide to Successful Living*, Melbourne, Nelson, 1986.

Menopause

Ballinger, S. and Walker, W. *Not The Change of Life—Breaking The Menopause Taboo*, Melbourne, Penguin Books, 1987.

INDEX